Joanna Hall

the WEIGHT LOSS BIBLE

Kyle Cathie Limited

First published in Great Britain in 2005 by
Kyle Cathie Limited, 122 Arlington Road, London NW1 7HP
email: general.enquiries@kyle-cathie.com
website: www.kylecathie.com

ISBN 1 85626 642 7
ISBN (13-digit) 978 1 85626 642 0

Text © 2005 Joanna Hall
www.joannahall.com

Photography © 2005 Dan Welldon
www.danwelldon.com
except: page 216 © Rob Lewine/CORBIS
page 123 © Vanessa Courtier

Project manager Gill Paul
Editorial assistant Vicki Murrell
Art direction and design Vanessa Courtier
Charts Ros Holder
Production Sha Huxtable and Alice Holloway
Recipes Louise Shaxson
Food styling Angela Boggiani and David Morgan
Hair and makeup Jane Tyler
Props stylist Wei Tang

Joanna Hall is hereby identified as the author of this work in accordance
with Section 77 of the Copyright, designs and Patents Act 1988.

A CIP catalogue record for this title is available from the British Library.

Colour separations by Scanhouse
Printed and bound in China by C & C Offset Printing Co., Ltd.

Contents

Introduction

Our weight has become a hot topic. So much so that we really can't escape it. Whether it's a serious item on the news about soaring obesity in the West, or a picture on the cover of a gossip magazine of a celebrity who's apparently ballooned overnight, the issue of weight is constantly demanding our attention. And if you think you've put on weight, you're not the only one: as a nation, we are getting fatter. What's to blame? A desk-bound day? Convenience foods? It's easy to point the finger at modern living, but just knowing what the problem might be won't get you anywhere. It's what you do about it that counts. You need a plan for action that's going to work. And although you probably haven't realised it, you've already started out on your weight loss journey by opening this book. You're on the right track at last.

Don't expect to find any quick-fix fad diets here. The only way to lose weight and to keep it off is basic physiology: cut back the calories and up your activity levels. Sounds simple, but of course it's not, as we all know. The key lies in getting the balance right so that it works effectively for you. I've designed *The Weight Loss Bible* to provide you with a step-by-step plan that works, helping you understand your body and get the most from it. After 12 years running weight management programmes – and dealing with real people who live real lives and have very real problems – I'm familiar with the enemies of weight reduction: there's defeatism, fatigue, stress and self-recrimination, to name just a very few. And there's just daily life – it gets in the way. Weight loss is a journey, and as with any journey there'll be high points and low points; there'll also be barriers blocking your path, but there are ways you can bash them down, as you'll see. And if you do fall by the wayside, don't worry: help is on hand to get you back on track. You'll find loads of plans, ideas and practical tips to stop yourself feeling frustrated and start feeling successful.

Before long, you'll realise you've become much more empowered; you'll have faith in your actions, and feel excited about what you can achieve. I've written *The Weight Loss Bible* for you to enjoy success, maintain your success, and feel confident in the knowledge that you've adopted a new, healthier way of living that won't just work for you today, but tomorrow as well, whatever your age or stage of life. And this is where the weight loss journey ends – this is your destination.

The steps you take, however small, will lead to big changes.

1 tell me about you

'How much weight will I lose?'

I bet this is the first question on your lips. But for successful weight loss, you need to ask yourself some other questions first!

The Weight Loss Bible will give you all the tools you need to achieve your goals, and show you how to use them, but whether you can do so effectively depends on you. You are the most important person on this journey of weight loss, and you come first — not your partner, not your boss. So before you start, you need to know exactly who it is you're dealing with.

Spending some time getting to know yourself a little better is an essential step, as the answers to the questions you ask yourself will have a direct effect on how you plan your journey as well as your rate of weight loss. This not only involves thinking about whether you exercise enough and what you eat, but also analysing your dieting history, since it will affect your expectations this time round.

And of course, there are other major factors you have to consider: your lifestyle and your personality. These — or rather your management of them — will have a key impact on your ability to get the weight off and keep it off (the hardest part). So although you may be champing at the bit to get going, take some time to do this groundwork first. Remember this is about you and your life — and how *you* can do this for *you*. If this approach makes you feel guilty, just remember: if you feel better about yourself, the other people around you will benefit too.

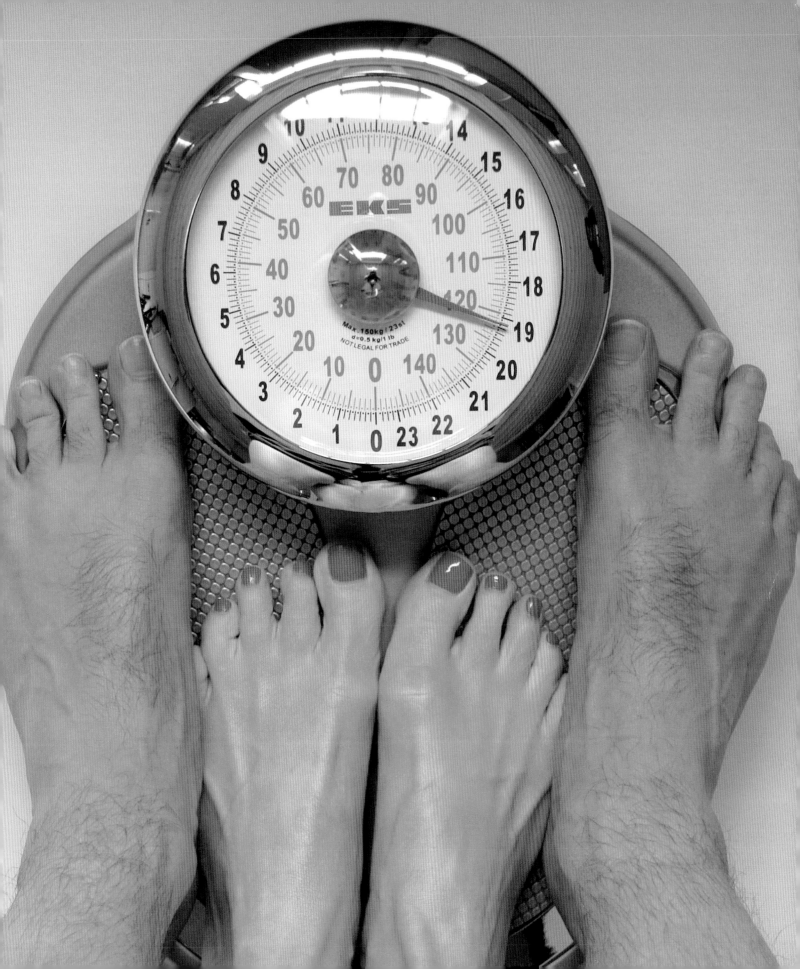

So let's get to know you...

Perhaps you think you have a pretty good idea of who you are, but the journey we are going on will require you to get to know yourself in quite a different way, almost as if you are another person; in fact, you will need to develop a 'relationship' with yourself. This involves taking a step back, and then a long, hard look at how your brain and your body work. You need to think about:

● how your weight has changed over the years
● what exercise you like or don't like to do
● what foods you like to eat
● why you like to eat
● when you eat fattening foods.

How many times have you beaten yourself up for eating a whole packet of biscuits? Or got really frustrated with yourself when you decided to go out with your friends instead of going to the gym – despite promising yourself you would do both? How often have you opted for the less healthy choice on the restaurant menu although you knew quite well what would be better for you? Getting cross with yourself, or despairing at your lack of willpower, will do little for your self-esteem, and can directly undermine your efforts. However, if you can see your own thought processes objectively – in effect, develop a relationship with your brain – you'll come to understand how it works. You'll see when it is hampering your efforts and, in time, this will give you more confidence, as you will be able to get the better of your negative thoughts. You'll come to trust yourself, and have faith in your abilities.

The bottom line
Many people want to lose weight to gain confidence – but you need to feel good about yourself NOW before you start losing weight. You must value yourself enough to really want to make the investment. The way you think about yourself can have just as powerful a role as the way you eat and the way you move your body. You need to train your brain and your body to work together in your fight against the flab.

Your dieting history

Realising an ambition involves a three-stage process – a THINKING stage, a RESOLVING stage, and a DOING stage. You think about it, you decide to do it and then you take the necessary action. So, weight loss should be easy! You:

- think about your shape and size and how to address them;
- decide on a plan of diet and exercise; and then
- take the appropriate steps to reach your weight loss goals.

It seems obvious that all these three things need to work in unison and go in the same direction… but are they happening? If you have struggled with your weight for a while and tried many different diets only to end up where you started, your body and your brain are undoubtedly out of tune.

Often we say we are going to take action, and we try to do what we said we would… but we still believe deep down that long-term success is beyond our reach, and that we will fail. We know only too well that we will find ourselves going through the same procedure again, possibly next month, next season or next New Year!

This sense of failure can often stem from things that we have experienced in the past. Our brain is focusing on times when success has eluded us – it's become very clever at developing what I call a 'Template of Failure'. This Template becomes a point of reference when we embark on a new challenge, thus undermining our self-esteem.

When you hit the inevitable challenges on your weight loss journey your Template of Failure kicks in, making it even harder for you to keep on track. Getting what you think, what you resolve to do and what you actually do to all work together is crucial for your success, but this won't happen if your thoughts are stuck on a Template of Failure. You need to start your weight loss journey from a Template of Success. In my experience, clients whose dieting history includes the quick-fix 'One Night Stand' often have a very pronounced Template of Failure. Each time you have opted for the One Night Stand – losing weight quickly, only to pile it back on again – your Template of Failure gets stronger.

BODY LAID BARE…

Ditch the ONE-NIGHT STAND! Successful weight loss is a lot like relationships. What we're looking for in a relationship – and what we're prepared to put into it – influence how it will turn out. Quick-fix diets are the one-night stands of the eating spectrum: in the same way as you realise that the night of passion with that person you fancied wasn't all you thought it would be, and your interest palls, the short-term weight loss you may have achieved doesn't last, and you come to see that the 'revolutionary' new diet has left you feeling exhausted, bad tempered, maybe with spots and bad breath, and above all, disappointed and feeding that Template of Failure. Compare this with a long-term relationship. A good, lasting partnership involves a bit of work and upkeep. It's not always glamorous, and there are inevitably problems along the way, but you know it feels right, and ultimately it works long-term. Over the years it will evolve, and it's the way in which you navigate the sometimes tricky road that determines the likelihood of long-term success. Your relationship with your body is exactly the same. Circumstances change, due to social and environmental factors, but the key is to be in tune with your brain so you can be responsive to your body's needs as they arise. So ditch that One-night Stand mentality now!

Change your Template of Failure to a Template of Success

The whole ethos of *The Weight Loss Bible* is about you achieving success, whatever may be happening in your life to make it difficult. Successfully navigating the challenges life throws your way is all part of the programme. A key to this is feeling confident – about yourself, and about the journey we're taking together – providing a firm foundation for your Template of Success. Don't worry; this can't miraculously happen overnight. But have faith in yourself, and in what we are doing, and it will strengthen your efforts. Work at it step by step, safe in the knowledge that everything is in place to support you. Let's start off by reinforcing some vital points. First of all, putting yourself first.

7 steps to raise your self-esteem

This section takes you through the strategies that will help you understand the importance of engaging not just your body but also your brain in your weight loss efforts. Each step builds upon the next, like the skin of an onion, taking you closer to the next layer and leading you towards your goal of creating a solid, stronger and more motivated whole.

Because each strategy builds the foundation for the next, you will need to go through each one methodically, and feel happy with it in order to progess. You may find some of the steps easier than others, but each is an important aspect of your journey to lose weight and keep it off.

This section isn't just something you'll read through once and forget about. As you go through life, there will be times when your weight fluctuates and your resolve falters, and you need to get back on track. You may well find that you need to revisit this section, because what was originally an easy strategy to master could, at a different time of your life, become more significant and challenging. It's not a bad idea to reaffirm your worth once a year by looking at the answers you gave to each of the seven exercises on the next pages when you last did them, and evaluating how much progress you have made in the intervening time. Why not dedicate a special self-esteem notebook for this purpose?

Feeling guilty or angry with yourself about minor day-to-day events is one thing, but if your whole life is dominated by negative emotions relating to something that has happened in the past, you may need the help of a counsellor or therapist to resolve the issues (contact the British Association of Counselling and Psychotherapy, www.bacp.co.uk). Remember: whatever you did then, and whatever you do now, you were, and are, doing the best you can in the circumstances.

1 Acknowledge your achievements

What you need to do: Acknowledge the great things you have accomplished in your life. Take credit for your accomplishments and don't belittle them by dismissing them as merely 'OK' or 'not bad'– use big, positive, bold words that truly reflect your achievements. Shout it out!

The logic: Too many of us down-play our triumphs, sometimes so others can feel more secure. At school we are taught to be modest, with the 'good' pupils promoting the others around them, never themselves. This modesty can actually undermine and sabotage confidence, because as we progress through our lives, fewer and fewer of us receive compliments or positive feedback on our performance. If you can't even acknowledge, let alone shout about, your own accomplishments, they go unnoticed by the most important person – YOU. And remember: if you don't value what you do, it's a cue for others to do the same.

2 List your successes

What you need to do: Make a list of all the things you decided you wanted to do in your life and then managed to accomplish. Include everything you can think of, from putting up shelves to passing your driving test to changing your own flat tyre or getting a promotion at work.

The logic: The action of recalling events or situations in which you have met a challenge builds your confidence: you have the ability to translate your thinking and saying into action.

3 Revisit past acts of bravery

What you need to do: If you are feeling demoralised or unable to face a situation for fear of rejection or failure, then recounting acts of bravery at other times or in other areas of your life can remind you that you are capable of confronting difficulties. To trigger these memories, sketch out a time line spanning from kindergarten to adult life. Try to jot down ten courageous acts. If you cannot remember, ask a friend or older member of the family. It doesn't matter how small – maybe it was deciding to own up to something when you were little, or going to a party where you knew your ex would be with his new girlfriend. Beside each event, write down the outcome of the event or situation.

The logic: Revisiting the past and citing even the smallest of brave acts can remind you of your bravery. As we get older our brain often forgets these small acts and instead we tend to focus on what we feel we have not been able to address and overcome. Even the most timid of people will have had fearless moments – the trick is to remind yourself.

4 Step into the TARDIS

What you need to do: Make a list of past situations or events that you were fearful of or worried about. Next, record how you dealt with the situation and decide whether you feel you handled it successfully or not. Finally, note how you think you could have improved the outcome by using a different approach or strategy.

The logic: Your attitude to weight management will involve a series of strategies and approaches to get the outcome you want. Looking at situations that have caused you hurt or problems in the past and how you have dealt with them requires you to assess your stategies. It also enables you to see that a desired outcome is not always immediate.

5 Think challenge, not problem

What you need to do: It's that old chestnut – is your glass half full or half empty? Whether you believe it or not, start telling yourself right now that it is half full. The more often you say it, the more you will come to believe it. Without getting evangelical, this new outlook will energise you, giving you the strength to get what you want.

The logic: How you view a situation can have a significant impact on how you deal with it. So stop looking at the difficulties life throws at you as 'problems', but instead see them as challenges that throw forward new ways for you to look at your situation and learn about yourself and others.

6 Be an early bird

What you need to do: Each day, aim to do the things you least want to do first. Leave the nice things until afterwards, like a child who leaves their favourite food on the plate till last. You will be able to deal with the things you would otherwise put off far more effectively, and your actions will empower you through other activities in your day.

The logic: This way, you no longer have something unpleasant hanging over you. Research shows also that we are better able to deal with challenging situations in the morning as levels of the stress hormones cortisol and adrenaline are naturally higher at this time. Make the most of your biochemicals!

7 Forgive yourself

What you need to do: Start right now by saying sorry to yourself. Say sorry for the way you have given yourself a hard time over an issue in your life, no matter how big or small. Perhaps you feel bad that you were late to pick up your child from school, or you feel that your lack of time and effort led to the breakdown of a relationship. Acknowledge why it happened and forgive yourself. Then move forward.

The logic: Criticising yourself is like telling your subconscious mind that you are a bad human being – and it will believe you. Everyone screws up sometimes, but the important thing is to acknowledge the error and move on. Negative emotions, such as depression, guilt and cynicism, were associated with higher abdominal fat distribution in a study at Pennsylvania State University because of their association with higher cortisol. Harbouring negative feelings won't help you achieve anything.

Like any relationship worth sustaining, the connection between your brain and body needs nurturing to remain strong. Don't neglect it. Acknowledge that sadness, fear and other negative emotions can be turned around so that they help you learn and heal, celebrate and get the most out of life.

Putting yourself on a pedestal

Right – we are going to play a game. This game is about finding out where you figure on your list of priorities. You'll need a pen and a piece of paper.

Write the numbers 1 to 7 down the left-hand side of the piece of paper. Decide who is the most important person in your life and write the name beside the number 1. After that, who is the next most important person in your life? Write the name beside the number 2. Ask yourself this question seven times, and write down your answers by each number in order.

How do you score this game? If you get to six or seven strikes and you don't see your name on the list, you are done for! Why? Because if you are that low down your priority list, then your weight loss attempts will fail. Your needs are not important enough for you to give them the time and energy they require. You do not value yourself enough.

Now ask yourself who is responsible for caring for all those other people who are more important than you. Chances are it is you. Let's get one thing straight: if you feel low about yourself, making sensible eating and other lifestyle choices becomes harder, and your health suffers. And don't think that it is just you that's affected. You don't just give yourself a hard time but also possibly jeopardise the smooth running of your family, your home and the very people you care about.

There's one thing that we have to establish before we go any further... you are not going to succeed in your weight loss journey unless your motivation is strong, and the best, truest motivation is the one that benefits you and you alone. Determining your true motivation is the the next step.

Take what you need Many people complain that they do not have enough time to eat healthily, take regular exercise and manage stress, but the issue is not always about making time. It is about taking time. Taking time is only possible when you feel you are worthy of it. Being happy to take time involves raising yourself a few rungs up the ladder. Even if you are not at the top of the list, getting higher is important. Taking time out is not about being selfish, it's about self-care.

The G spot motivation

Open any women's magazine and you'll be reminded that finding your G spot heightens your enjoyment of sex. It's something that both you and your partner will want to do, since once you enjoy something, you start to want more.

If you want to lose weight you need to find your G spot for weight loss. What is your long-term motivation to keep your size down? For many, finding your true G spot for weight loss, as in sex, can be difficult. And it's no good having some vague idea and faking it. In the end it'll give you no satisfaction at all.

What is your current motivation? It may be to lose weight for a summer holiday with your best friend, a special occasion or perhaps even your wedding day. These are short-lived – you haven't quite got there. If you really want to slim, you have to come up with something that will give you lasting pleasure, and keep those inches off for life.

Ask yourself what you really want to achieve with your weight loss. What is it about being slimmer that you think will make you ultimately happier, ultimately more fulfilled? Maybe it's social confidence, or perhaps the freedom to wear what you want. Or perhaps feeling fitter and having the freedom to do more will give you lasting satisfaction? Think about it.

1 Write down your previous motivations for wanting to lose weight

What you need to do: So you have tried dozens of diets in the past. For each time you have started a new diet I want you to write down your motivation for trying it. Next to each motivation, make a note of whether you felt your G spot motivation was large or small.

The logic: To see what motivates you to lose weight, and thus discover what and how big your G spot motivation is. You may find that by adding small G spots together you can create one bigger one.

2 Recall other times when you were motivated

What you need to do: Think back to an event or period when you were truly driven to do something – perhaps it was to get through your professional qualifications, recover from an operation, or plan a surprise party for someone. Whatever it was, you were strongly motivated to make it happen.

The logic: Realise that if you were strong enough to have the motivation to accomplish those achievements, then you have the ability to apply the same strength to losing weight. Tap into that motivational strength and you can use it to help you reach your goal.

3 Start to heal yourself

What you need to do: This is a simple game to help you identify how large your G spot motivation is. Make two lists: in the first, make a note of all your harmful lifestyle habits, and in the second, think of a healing substitute. Now decide which harmful habits you are prepared to replace with the things that are ultimately going to get you what you want. Next, ask yourself how long you are prepared to do this for – is it a day, a week, a fortnight, a month, or longer?

The logic: If you're only prepared to do this for a short period, it looks like you'll never be really satisfied with the result. Otherwise, wow! You'll never look back.

One of the main problems is that we all want to lose weight and we want to lose it now, this minute. Your efforts *will* be rewarded, but there will always be a gap in time between the effort you make and the rewards your receive. *The Weight Loss Bible* will help you with the planning, and support you by anticipating where you may need some extra help. If you follow the guidance in this book, you'll find a lot of the hard work has been taken out.

Setting your goals

The essential point with goal-setting is to make sure your target is realistic and achievable. A lot has been written about goal-setting and weight loss and with good reason, because so many difficulties can arise if your goal is unachievable within the time set. Realistic weight loss is around 1kg (2¼lbs) a week – although this will depend on your dieting history, the consistency of your effort and your own metabolism. Your rate of change will vary but as a rule of thumb it is not unrealistic to be able to drop a clothes size in four weeks. Aiming for a weight loss of 1kg a week is sensible; however, bear in mind the rate at which you lose it may not be consistent.

Think about this: Remember your weight five years ago – and imagine a straight line from there to here, the present moment. Logically, then, you can extend that line and see where you'll be where in five years' time if you continue with your current eating and exercise habits. If that place isn't where you want to be with your body, your health and your shape, then you need to address your thoughts, decisions and actions right now. The present is on the same straight line as the past and future, so if you want to change direction, act now. You can do this.

Barrier bashing

On your weight-loss journey you are going to come up against a whole host of barriers that can hinder your efforts. Many will be genuine challenges, possibly the same ones that have hindered your progress in the past. So deciding on a way to deal with them and bash them down will be part of your weight loss tool kit. The logic concerning barriers is simple: when they are high, or perceived to be high, then confidence is low. Identifying your barriers in advance and learning how to bash them down will help keep you on track. As you follow *The Weight Loss Bible* you'll come across several barriers, but you'll also find ways to help you become a great Barrier Basher! Remember: if you do not attempt to implement some of the action plans to break the barriers down, then your barrier still exists. Learning to bash down your barriers can help you to become an Inner Coach rather than an Inner Critic.

Barrier: Lack of time

Probably the most cited barrier. You don't need to have hours on end to take action, or put your normal life on hold to make weight loss work for you.

Bash it down: Exercise earlier in the day. Studies have shown that people who are new to exercise and choose to exercise first thing in the morning are 75 per cent more likely to still be exercising 12 months later. Schedule in exercise blocks at the start of each week and write reminders everywhere – on your computer screen, diary, mobile phone and post-it notes – to let you know when you should be exercising. Think shorter exercise bouts, not longer! Research has shown that people who take shorter exercise bouts end up completing more than those whose exercise bouts were longer (*International Journal of Obesity*, 1995). Seek out ways to exercise at home. People tend to stick with home-based exercises more than facility-based exercise sessions (Perri et al., 1997).

Barrier: Too much effort

Many people perceive exercise as a skill, requiring great physical co-ordination or an aptitude for sport – but this needn't be the case.

Bash it down: Seek out ways to exercise at home. For example, use home exercise DVDs, or try walking routes of differing lengths near your home. Stop looking at exercise purely as a way of getting hot and sweaty, or as something that has to be done in exercise kit. Building up Lifestyle Activity to top up your Structured Exercise can help change your traditional perceptions about exercise.

Barrier: Lack of support

Social support is very important, whether it is from a partner, friend or support group. There will be people, however, who actively discourage your new healthy habits.

Bash it down: Seek out and identify who will be the supporters and saboteurs. Studies with recovering heart disease patients reveal that men had an 80 per cent adherence rate to their exercise programme when supported by their spouse compared to 40 per cent when their spouse had a neutral attitude.

Find exercise partners who will be powerful motivational supporters. Find people who can help make it easier to build exercise into your life. For example, if your partner or friend agrees to pick up the children three days a week, you can use that time to exercise. Explaining to others the importance to you of following your exercise and eating programme may help them be more supportive.

Barrier: Lack of self-esteem

Building self-confidence in yourself right now is crucial. Don't wait for your self-confidence to suddenly appear once you have lost weight. Invest in it now.

Bash it down: Teach yourself small successes. Take 120 micro-bouts of 15 seconds' exercise throughout the day and you've done 30 minutes of exercise without even realising it. Congratulate yourself with post-it reminders each time you complete your actions. Regularly re-visit the steps to self-esteem on pages 18–19.

Barrier: Lack of knowledge

You want to lose weight but you don't know where to start, what plan to follow, what exercise to do or what food to eat. A lack of knowledge can be just as confusing as having too much information and not knowing where to start.

Bash it down: Make a commitment to learning about how your body works and the impact your actions, however small, can have. Invest in yourself and read the relevant sections in *The Weight Loss Bible*. Enrol on a course with a qualified personal trainer or weight management support group.

Be specific about what you want to achieve, so your plan can be as appropriate as possible.

Barrier: Too many obstacles

Hindrances such as not being near a health club or having to work late, the menstrual cycle or a weekend away with friends can all be hindrances or obstacles that act as a barrier.

Bash it down: Honestly identify your behaviour chains. These are the chains of events that can stop you from exercising or eating sensibly. For example, you may have planned to go to the gym after work but you ended up not going because your boss shoved a report under your nose as you were walking out the door and said he wanted it ready for first thing the following morning. You may blame your lack of gym attendance on the actions of your boss, but in actual fact, the real reason could be because you overslept, which put pressure on your day from the start.

What is success?

Measuring your success plays a very important part in sustaining your weight loss motivation. But what constitutes success? Success may primarily mean victory on the scales, but your success will also be reflected in a far wider range of changes than this – and learning about them now will be helpful when your weight loss slows down or even stays the same for a while, despite your continued efforts. (This is quite normal; it should be something you're prepared for.)

Positive side-effects of weight loss success will include having more energy, sleeping better, reducing high blood pressure or blood cholesterol, dropping belt buckle-holes, increased confidence, noticing a more radiant complexion and a spring in your step, and not feeling short of breath as you walk up the stairs... The list is endless, so note down your own particular successes. There will be far more than just the decreasing measurements on your bathroom scales.

We've had a look at your mental shape; now let's look at your physical shape...

2 where are you now?

You have got to know yourself a little better, and you are all ready to go. But do you know the point you're starting from? What kind of shape is your body in at the moment? This chapter is all about finding out.

Do I really need to know?

Yes. Establishing what shape you're in now will give you a baseline that you can use as your starting point. Many of my clients find the process of taking initial measurements daunting, but try not to be put off as you do need to measure your progress. There will be times on your weight loss journey when your motivation may wane or you may feel a little despondent, so it's useful to have a record of your starting-point to hand, so you can see just how far you've come. Studies have shown conclusively that the more accountable weight loss participants are, the more successful their outcome. So self-monitoring is a crucial part.

What do I measure?

I would strongly encourage you to measure both your body shape and your body composition, and there is a number of ways you can do this. Some methods are simpler than others, so choose the one that you feel best able to work with. Many have different definitions and thresholds of obesity, which can often lead to confusion when you are trying to establish whether or not you fall within a healthy range.

Your body is made up of lean muscle tissue and adipose (fat) tissue around a skeleton, which forms a framework for your body shape. From a health perspective, the most significant factor is the amount of adipose tissue you have. Our bodies hold adipose fat internally around delicate organs such as the liver, kidneys and heart and, more visibly, it is also stored under the surface of the skin and on top of the muscles, which lie over our skeletal framework. Some adipose tissue is also stored inside our muscles. If you are putting on weight, this will be most apparent in the fat deposits of the adipose tissue under the skin; however, additional fat will also be stored around our delicate organs and in our muscles, posing some serious health risks.

How often should I measure?

This is up to you, and partly depends upon what suits you and what will most effectively support you and keep you on track on your weight loss journey. As a rule I encourage my clients to use one simple form of measurement once a week and another more comprehensive system once a month. For example, weigh yourself once a week and take a set of body circumference measurements on the first day of each month. And ladies, remember: a woman can put on up to 2kg (4lb) at the time of her period just through fluid retention.

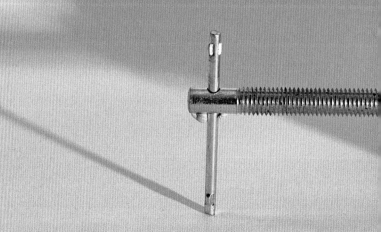

When should I measure?

Again this is up to you, but in my experience the start of the week is the best time. This helps prevent you from splurging during your leisure time at the weekend and also serves to focus you for the week ahead. Whether you measure first thing in the morning or later in the day will make no difference to your overall weight loss progression – the important thing is to measure at the same time each time, either without clothes or wearing the same garments. Some measurements take into account your body's water content, so time of day may be specific to them. Measuring at the same time will give you a proper yardstick, allowing you to observe a true change.

Obesity and your health – the hard facts

Obesity predisposes you to a whole realm of life-threatening diseases. There's unequivocal statistical proof of an increased risk of developing dozens of disorders. Your risk of suffering from coronary heart disease increases by 30 per cent, and obesity accounts for 75 per cent of new cases of Type 2 diabetes. It can steal up to a decade off your life expectancy and also has a major impact on the quality of your life. If you are obese, you are at more risk of the following:

Cardiovascular system: hypertension, coronary heart disease, varicose veins, stroke, deep vein thrombosis

Breast: breast cancer (or gynaecomastia in men)

Reproductive system: endometrial cancer, cervical cancer, menstrual irregularities, polycystic ovarian syndrome, altered sex hormones, prostate cancer in men

Urological system: stress incontinence

Respiratory system: breathlessness, sleep apnoea

Skin: sweat rashes, fungal infections, lymphoedema, cellulitis

Skeleton: osteoarthritis, gout

Gastrointestinal system: hiatus hernia, gallstones, fatty liver and cirrhosis, colorectal cancer, haemorrhoids

Endocrine system: reduced growth hormone and prolactin, hyperlipidaemia, insulin resistance, diabetes mellitus

Neurological system: nerve entrapment, neural tube defects

Pregnancy: obstetric complications, Caesarian section

Systems of measurement

There is a wide variety of systems available, each of them measuring a different aspect of body fat and with varying degrees of accuracy. This helps to explain why somebody may be classified as having a healthy weight according to one system but overweight according to another. Obviously this can prove confusing, so although you may be interested to see how you compare using all the methods of measurement, I suggest that you select just one or two, and be consistent with your measuring.

The bathroom scales

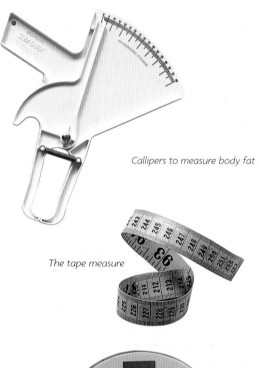

Callipers to measure body fat

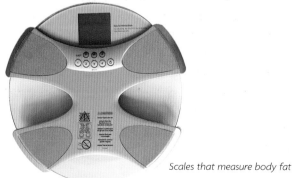

The tape measure

The bathroom scales

What they do Show you how much you weigh.

The healthy range It is difficult to give healthy range targets, although a 5–10 per cent decrease in excess weight can lead to a significantly reduced risk of chronic disease and disability. Use scales in conjunction with your BMI or waist circumference to give you a healthy range to work towards.

The drawbacks Since they account for the weight of your muscle, fat and skeletal system as a whole they do not tell you the amount of body fat you have or its distribution.

The benefits One of the easiest measures to take (and of course, the most widely used). Just be brave and stand on a set of good, calibrated scales.

Body Mass Index (BMI)

What it does BMI measures your weight in relation to your height. To establish your BMI, measure your height in metres and your weight in kilograms, and then divide your weight by your height squared:

$W \div H^2 = BMI$

For example, you weigh 63kg (10 stone) and are 1.70m (5ft 7in) tall.

1.70 x 1.70 = 2.89

63 ÷ 2.89 = 21.79

The healthy range A normal BMI should fall between 18.5 and 24.9. Anything between 24.9 and 29.9 is considered overweight and above that qualifies as obese. Once you know

Scales that measure body fat

your weight and height you can get your BMI automatically calculated at www.joannahall.com.

The drawbacks The BMI does not distinguish between fat and muscle, nor does it take into account where your body fat is distributed. This is important because it is not just the amount or the composition of excess weight that affects health, but its regional distribution – where the extra fat is stored within the body. It's also not a good measure of progress as you get fitter, since increased muscle mass may actually make you heavier, although you will be substantially leaner and trimmer, and your clothes will fit better.

The benefits The BMI is a widely used measurement of obesity. Many GPs and medical establishments talk about BMI, so knowing your BMI score is useful.

Waist circumference

What it does Measures round your middle (a normal tape measure will do).

The healthy range It has been suggested that if waist circumference rises above 90cm (35$\frac{1}{2}$in) in men and above 80cm (31$\frac{1}{2}$in) in women, the risk of metabolic complications is increased. Weight reduction is strongly advised if waist circumference is more than 102cm (40in) in men and 88cm (35in) in women, as this represents a significantly increased medical risk.

The drawbacks Reduction in waist circumference may take some time to materialise, so it's advisable to use this method in conjunction with another body measurement that may be more sensitive to changes, such as weight. It has been recommended that sex-specific waist circumference cut-off points need to be developed for different populations because people from different ethnic backgrounds vary in their level of risk for diseases such as coronary heart disease and Type 2 diabetes (*World Health Organisation, 2000*).

The benefits Very easy to do. Recent evidence suggests that waist circumference on its own may prove very useful. It correlates closely with BMI and WHR (see below) and is a good index of intra-abdominal fat mass and total body fat.

Waist-to-hip ratio (WHR)

What it does Identifies patients with abdominal fat accumulation. It is a recognised clinical method by which the waist is measured at the narrowest point and the hips are measured at the widest point. The waist measurement is then divided by the hip measurement.

The healthy range A high WHR is defined as above 1.0 in men and above 0.85 in women. A healthy range is below these two values.

The drawbacks Like waist circumference, WHR only identifies the distribution of your abdominal fat, so it's wise to use it in conjunction with another, more sensitive measure.

The benefits Like waist circumference, it's easy to do, using a simple tape measure.

Percentage body fat

What it does Calculates the amount of fat your body contains in relation to your muscle mass.

The healthy range This depends on your age. For adults between 18 and 40, the healthy ranges are 18–26 per cent for men and 24–34 per cent for women.

The drawbacks A number of methods can be used to gauge percentage body fat, some more accurate than others. Underwater weighing is the most exact, although this is expensive and not widely available. More convenient methods include using hand-held callipers to take measurements at three to six sites on the body and then feeding these figures into a regression equation. Simpler still, you can stand on a set of special scales using a non-invasive technique called bioelectrical impedence. The scales can be used privately in your home, whereas the calliper method needs to be administered by a trained professional.

The benefits If you know your weight and your body fat percentage you can easily work out the weight of your fat and muscle, known as fat free mass and lean muscle mass respectively. Specially made scales available to measure children's body fat can be useful to avoid embarrassment in a clinical setting.

Girth measurements

What it does Measures body circumference at specific points (with a tape measure):

Chest across the nipple line

Waist around the narrowest part of your midriff

Navel around the midriff, directly over the bellybutton

Hips across the top of the buttock cheeks. This may not necessarily be the widest part of your hips.

Thighs 20cm (8in) up from top of your kneecaps, standing with your feet together. (You will need some help when taking this measurement.)

Chest

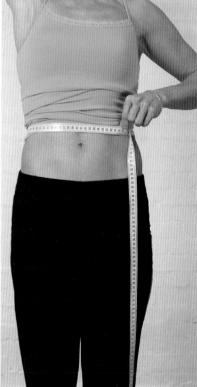

Waist

The healthy range Except for the waist circumference measurement guidelines on page 31, there are no standard recognised reference ranges.

The drawbacks You may need some help to check that you are positioning the tape correctly.

The benefits Simple and cheap to do. Measuring at various sites can be more motivating, as different hormone distribution and concentration in different parts of the body will mean your body may change shape more in one part than another. Remember: any scrap of change is encouraging!

Keep it simple If you're still not sure which measuring system to use, my advice would be to keep it simple. Monitor your weight and either your waist measurement and/or girth measurements. And if even this feels unmanageable, I always think the old blue jeans measure – although not scientifically sound – can in many ways be the most personally powerful. Dig out that favourite piece of clothing that you can't fit into any more, and use that as your monthly reference point.

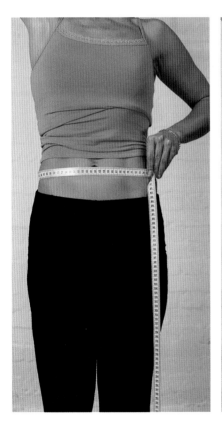

Navel

Hips

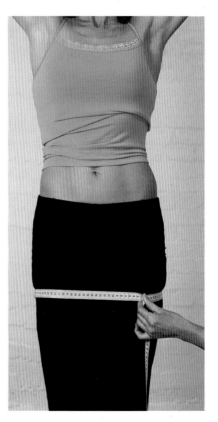

Thighs

Body shape

We have become so used to seeing incredible celebrity body transformations on television and in magazines that we seem to expect the same level of transformation from our own body. In reality, however, most of us don't have the sort of money it takes — or the luxury of air-brushing. It is possible to improve our figures but exactly how much can we change the body shape Mother Nature dealt us?

Our fundamental body shape — skeletal frame, muscle, body fat and distribution of certain hormones — is determined by our genes. According to geneticist Claude Bouchaud, our genes and the hormones we produce during puberty can determine our body shape by as much as 70 per cent... so that leaves about 30 per cent that can be redefined, moulded and determined by exercise and what we eat.

As we get older our bodies naturally lose muscle, but muscle tone can be improved and muscle size can be increased with appropriate exercise. Body fat is directly determined by energy balance — consuming too many calories and not expending them increases body fat, while expending more calories than are consumed encourages body fat reduction. But unless we undergo significant cosmetic surgery, which is a very bad idea, our basic body shape — whether we're 'big-boned' or 'petite' — is pretty fixed.

We generally fall into four broad body shapes. I've categorised them as: pear, red pepper, carrot and apple.

What shape are you?

You are more pear if:
- your hips are wider than your shoulders
- you have a smaller upper body frame
- your top half is 1 to 2 dress sizes smaller than your lower half.

You are more red pepper if:
- you have an ample bottom and bust with a defined waist
- you are a classic hourglass shape
- you are prone to gaining weight and storing body fat on arms and legs.

You are more carrot if:
- you have broadish shoulders with slimmer hips
- you have a smallish bottom and bust
- you tend not to hold excess fat around your midriff
- your waistline is not clearly defined

You are more apple if:
- you store body fat around your midriff rather than hips and thighs
- you are shorter in height
- you have a flattish bottom.

What's your body frame?

Here is a quick way to identify the size of your body frame –
it's not scientifically proven but it will give you a rough idea.

Encircle your wrist with your thumb and middle finger.
If the middle finger overlaps your thumb, chances are you are
small-framed. If the middle finger and thumb touch, you have
a medium-sized body frame; and if the finger and thumb do
not touch you are more likely to have a larger frame.

Remember: for optimum health all body types need a
balanced exercise programme involving a combination of
cardiovascular, resistance and flexibility work. But a particular
type may benefit from extra concentration on a specific
component. As you continue on your weight loss journey and
follow your appropriate plan, you'll see a specially designed
workout for your body shape.

BODY LAID BARE...

How hormones affect our shape Some of us store more body fat on our hips and thighs while others tend to have long lean arms and
legs but store more body fat around our midriffs. This distribution of fat is associated directly with two main hormones: lipoprotein lipase, or
LPL, which encourages fat storage, and hormone-sensitive lipase, or HSL, which encourages fat to be distributed in the blood and then burnt
off. The amount of LPL and HSL may vary from person to person and from one part of the body to another, directly affecting our shape.
• More LPL in the belly and less HSL in the lower hip area creates an apple-like shape, with more body fat distributed around the belly.
• More LPL in the hips and backs of the arms and less HSL in the upper body produces a pear-like shape.
This hormone distribution helps to explain why we still retain the same overall body shape when we lose weight.

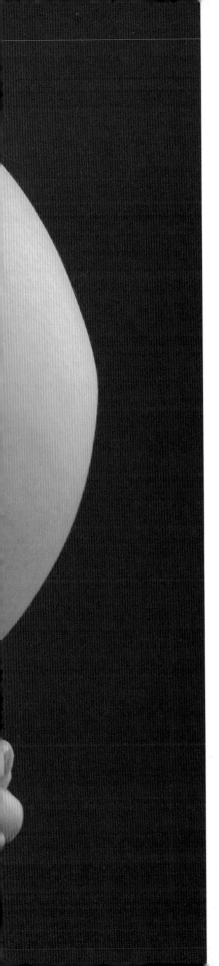

The life journey of a body

As your body accompanies you through life, certain biological changes will occur at particular stages that affect your shape and weight. A sedentary lifestyle and excessive calorie intake can compound their effects. Recognising these changes will help you develop an understanding of your body and how it responds on your weight loss journey, and this will further enhance the relationship you have with your body and your brain. You'll find information about changes during childhood and puberty in Chapter Seven.

20s

Studies have shown that from the age of 25 our aerobic capacity decreases by 1–2 per cent each year. This means your heart and lungs have to work harder to complete everyday tasks, although you may not feel it until you have to overexert yourself – running for a bus, or dashing up several flights of stairs to answer the phone, for instance.

Pregnancy

During pregnancy you gain weight and you need to gain weight. This results from a change in the concentration of hormones your body produces as well as from the growing baby and amniotic fluid inside. A woman of average build will put on around 10–12kg (20–24lb), mostly around the abdomen. If you find you are putting on much more weight than this (or not so much), then consult your doctor.

30s

After the age of 30 the body secretes less growth hormone, stimulating a loss of lean body tissue and encouraging greater storage of fat. In this decade, women lose 140–170g (5–6oz) of muscle mass a year and can gain as much, if not more, fat mass. If you are not doing any weight-bearing activity by the age of 39 you could potentially have lost 1.8kg (4lb) of muscle mass and replaced it with body fat, slowing your metabolism down still more, and putting you on the slippery road to further weight gain. Men are also likely to lose a lot of muscle mass in this decade if they don't maintain a high level of physical activity, and they are more prone to putting on weight round their abdomens (becoming apple-shaped).

40s

Peri-menopause is defined as the time leading up to menopause (it may start as early as ten years before menstruation ceases) and is marked by a fluctuation of hormones. Women at this stage experience a decrease in their metabolic rate owing to changes in hormones and muscle mass. Oestrogen levels become erratic, waxing and waning, and the storage site for fat shifts to your middle, around your abdomen. During peri-menopause many women experience mood swings, memory loss, bone loss, cholesterol changes, hot flushes and sleep disturbances, all of which may affect your self-esteem and motivation to keep physically active. Men will also notice signs of their metabolism decreasing.

50s

Menopause is defined as the 12 months after a woman's last period, usually around the age of 52. After menopause women lose about 66 per cent of oestrogen and 50–60 per cent of testosterone. The oestrogen tends to decline at a faster rate than the testosterone and encourages a redistribution of body fat. In most cases it is redistributed from the hips to the middle section and blood pressure and cholesterol levels rise. All these changes can put women at a higher risk of cardiovascular disorders, but it is overweight men who now find themselves in a real danger zone at this age. Consult your doctor before starting a new fitness or weight loss programme in this age group.

60s+

Activity that focuses on balance, mobility and flexibility is especially important to help maintain posture and stability and safeguard against falls. Decline in physical activity levels with age is not inevitable and maintaining them can play an important part in the prevention of strokes, osteoporosis and arthritis. At this age your daily nutritional energy needs start to lower as your muscle mass will be less than at younger ages. However, getting a variety of food and maintaining your nutrient base is still vitally important, both for energy and for maintaining healthy weight. Daily walking and balance exercises can be simple but effective health investments for you and the quality of your life.

Factors that may affect weight loss

It's possible that in the past you've found it unusually hard to shift those pounds. There may be reasons for this, and we'll have a look at some of them here. Understanding these forces can relieve the burden of guilt and point the way forward to effective weight management solutions, strengthening the relationship between our brains and our bodies and weakening that Template of Failure.

Genes

We've already seen that our genes may account for up to 70 per cent of our body shape, which leaves about 30 per cent we can potentially change. This is because certain genes affect metabolism and/or eating behaviour, and therefore influence body mass and fat. They create a complex interplay of physiological processes that can affect our shape, rate of weight loss and appetite. While obesity is not inevitable, some people may be battling against a biological inheritance.

Modern living

It is now generally agreed that the fundamental causes of the obesity epidemic in the Western world are sedentary lifestyles and high-fat, energy-dense diets – products of the profound changes taking place in our society. The ever-increasing demands of the workplace mean that fewer people have time to cook fresh food; others are unaware of the hidden calories in convenience foods.

Hunger drive

Our appetite mechanism originated in prehistory with our human forebears who lived in a harsh environment, hunting animals and gathering plants for food. They needed a healthy appetite – especially for calorifically dense foods – to ensure that they stored enough energy to keep them going through leaner times. This hunger drive was so essential for survival that some anthropologists believe there is an evolutionary residue, which, in the sedentary, food-rich Western world, often leads us to gain excess weight. It may not only affect our appetite but also regulate how efficiently we convert food into energy.

Calcium deficiency

One evolutionary factor associated with obesity is calcium levels. Studies by the US government, among others, show that people with higher levels of calcium have more control over their body weight. When calcium is abundant in the body, it appears that fat is used for energy. When calcium levels drop the body may shift into survival mode, encouraging increased fat storage.

Insulin resistance

Hormones are complex molecules produced by the endocrine glands that manage many bodily functions and processes. Insulin, known as the 'hunger hormone', influences the amount

Get naked: Develop a relationship with your cells. Go on – take your clothes off right now and stand in front of a full-length mirror. YES, right now. Give yourself a good long hard look and say: '*If I want to see a change in my body shape [a leaner body, slimmer thighs or whatever your goals may be], I need to develop a relationship with my body and specifically a relationship with my cells.*'
Your cells are tiny microscopic units in your body that carry out your everyday needs, and are responsible for using your body's energy effectively and the food you eat efficiently. Developing a good relationship with your cells is like a friendship; if you treat them well then they repay your kindness. If, on the other hand, you go on erratic starvation diets and suddenly start exercising excessively, your cells will be confused and will not know how to respond. The net result will be that your energy will flag and your weight loss efforts start to flounder, despite what you perceive as putting in masses of hard work. So be kind to your cells – they want to help you.

of body fat we store by inhibiting food intake, increasing energy expenditure and regulating the amount of glucose (a sugar) in the blood. However, if a person is significantly overweight and consumes large amounts of refined ('simple') carbohydrates, this can result in the condition known as insulin resistance. A person with insulin resistance has to produce more insulin to reduce their blood glucose to normal levels, and so their satiety lever is never pushed (meaning they never feel full). Insulin resistance often leads to obesity, and both are major triggers of Type 2 diabetes.

Stress hormones

Stress – whether physical or psychological – can wreak havoc with weight control by releasing the so-called 'stress hormones' to deal with what the body perceives as an emergency. If stress is keeping you awake at night, your cortisol levels increase, encouraging the body to switch to a fat-storing mode. Studies on animals and humans have demonstrated that depriving them of sleep increased both appetite and food consumption. If you don't think you can reduce your stress levels yourself, through exercise, or perhaps meditation, then see your doctor.

The winter months

The time of year also may affect appetite. Many people get depressed in the late autumn and winter, when there is less sunlight, and often tend to eat more. This condition is called Seasonal Affective Disorder (SAD). Even those people who do not suffer from SAD are often impelled by the colder weather to prefer heavy, hot foods instead of salads.

BODY LAID BARE...

Is stress making you fat? Some people thrive on stress, undertaking great challenges and reaching for the stars. Many of us, however, react to pressure by reaching for a bag of chocolate cookies. The relationship between stress and eating is complicated. Does stress simply reduce our willpower to make good food choices or does it actually increase our appetites?

The human stress response is intended as a short-term solution to an immediate problem, but we seldom face the kind of dangers that would require such a response. Our modern enemies are overloaded schedules, belligerent bosses, traffic jams, financial pressures and a host of other worries. They are formidable and can be deadly over the decades.

When faced with a stressful situation, our brains signal an acute immediate response causing the adrenal glands to release a hormone called cortisol. High levels of cortisol result in increased appetite and fat deposits. When stress is chronic and long-term, cortisol levels can remain elevated for long periods of time. This leads to increased body fat around the waist, higher blood pressure and blood sugar imbalances; further effects may include a vicious cycle of hormone imbalances linked to cardiac dysfunction and increased obesity.

Stress makes us crave foods that are calorie-laden and contain few nutrients. No definitive research has determined why stress-eaters make bad food choices. Some desire high-energy foods containing sugar, especially chocolate. Others prefer salty foods like crisps, chips, popcorn and crackers. Many overeat at the first signs of stress, while others initially shun food. However, after some initial weight loss from this reduction in food intake, approximately 40 per cent of people typically begin to eat excessively 6 to 7 weeks later, and ultimately weigh in above their original weight.

So now you know what shape you're in and what you're up against – we've come a long way already. With both your brain and your body working together, we're ready to go on to the next stage, and find out what you need to do.

3what you need to do

The Energy Gap

Now you've had a good look at both your brain and your body, you know where you are and what you're

dealing with. What we're going to do next is to arm you with the tools you need to continue your weight

loss journey. This entails simplifying all the information you need and putting it into a useable form that you

can slot into your life. We'll start with the basic principle for weight loss – the Energy Gap. If you want to

lose weight you have to create an Energy Gap – put simply, you have to expend more calories through

moving your body than you consume through food and drink. The bigger the Energy Gap, the more weight

you lose. It's that simple. And if you can sustain the gap, the greater your long-term success will be.

How to create an Energy Gap

As we all know, what we eat is commonly referred to as our diet. While I am not keen on that word – as people say they are 'on a diet', it has acquired connotations of deprivation and starvation – it has become such a widely used term that it is the easiest way to refer to your choice of food. Let me stress, however, that you should not be feeling deprived; enjoying your food is a central part of your ongoing weight loss success, and we'll be looking at this in Chapter 5. How you move your body I refer to as physical activity, and this broadly falls into three categories:

- Lifestyle Activity
- Occupational Activity
- Structured Exercise

In this chapter you will see that much of the most effective physical activity for long-term weight management isn't difficult or vigorous, but it does need to be done consistently.

What is a calorie?

Look at any food label and you will see the terms Kcals (kilocalories) or Kjoules (kilojoules). These are units of energy. 'Calorie' is the most widely used term while 'kilojoule' is more often used in research. We'll use calories here, but if you need to convert an energy value, remember 1 kilocalorie = 4.2 kilojoules.

Will I always be counting calories?

No – don't panic, you won't. Studies have shown that people who are able to control their weight long-term do not count calories, although they are calorie-aware. When you start out on your weight loss journey, knowing the basics can be very empowering and will help you make better choices when it comes to food and exercise. This in turn will strengthen your own personal Template of Success. Applying this knowledge will gradually become second nature as you develop healthier lifestyle choices.

To lose a pound of fat

Losing a pound (0.45kg) of fat requires creating an Energy Gap of 3,500 calories. So if you want to lose 1lb in a week, that means reducing your intake by 500 calories each day. In theory you could just eat small quantities of ice-cream and sweets and still lose weight, as long as your calorie intake is less than calories burnt. But before you leap for joy and head off to the corner shop, here's a word of warning: in the long term, choosing fruits, vegetables, whole grains and good sources of protein instead will not only facilitate weight management and prevent weight regain, but it will also ensure that you look and feel better. Choosing a diet that results in a permanent lifestyle change is essential for success. You will find the Recipes and Menu Plans in Chapter 5 very helpful for getting you on track. You'll soon realise that you can enjoy healthy foods just as much as the things you crave at the moment.

How your body uses energy

Your body is constantly expending energy in different ways:

- The energy we need to function – for breathing, or for keeping our hearts beating, for example – is referred to as Resting Metabolic Rate (RMR).
- The energy we use to process our food – the digesting, absorbing, metabolising and storing of nutrients – is called the Thermic Effect of Food.
- And the energy we use as we move around – be it Structured Exercise, Occupational Activity and Lifestyle Activity – is called the Thermic Effect of Exercise.

These three energy forms add up to total energy expenditure. Discovering how each one relates to your overall energy expenditure will help you create your Energy Gap.

Mind the gap Ensure you are regularly expending more calories through physical activity than you are consuming in food. If you Mind the Energy Gap, your weight will look after itself.

24-hour Activity Chart

am	24	1	2	3	4	5	6	7	8	9	10	11	12	13	14	15	16	17	18	19	20	21	22	23	pm

Think of your typical day as you colour in this chart

- Colour in black the time you are lying down (sleeping, napping or stretched out on the sofa).
- Colour in red all the time you are sitting (at work, in a vehicle, at home; include such things as watching TV, reading, at a desk or computer, eating, and all sedentary leisure activities).
- Colour in orange the time you are on your feet (doing light activities in your day).
- Colour in yellow the time you are doing strength or resistance work (include heavy manual lifting).
- Colour in green the time you are doing moderately intense physical activity (such as brisk walking).
- Colour in purple the time you are doing vigorous physical activity (such as running).

BODY LAID BARE...

How *they* compare Your *Resting Metabolic Rate* has the greatest potential impact on your total energy expenditure, accounting for 65 to 75 per cent of the energy your body burns. Your RMR is strongly linked to the amount of muscle mass you have. A pound of muscle will burn between 50 and 60 calories a day whilst a pound of fat burns fewer than 10. Surprisingly, very low calorie diets (less than 1,100 to 1,200 kcal per day for women, 1,400 to 1,500 kcal per day for men) have been associated with a reduction in RMR. This reduction can actually encourage your body to store fat rather than burn it - not what you want to happen.

The *Thermic Effect of Food* requires approximately 10 per cent of the energy consumed at any one sitting, and is the smallest contributor to total energy expenditure.

The *Thermic Effect of Exercise* is the most variable component of total energy expenditure, as it depends on your level of daily activity. Absolutely anyone can increase their total energy expenditure – whether you like to stick on your training shoes or not.

How active do you think you are?

Ask someone if they have an active life, and they'll most probably tell you how busy their day has been. But think about it. Okay, so you may feel tired in the evening, but is it because you were mentally, geographically or physically active? Here's what I mean. You take the kids to school, finish off a report, get the washing done, take a parcel to the post office, pick up a prescription from the doctor, do half a day at the office, pick up the kids at 4pm, take Johnny to football, Elizabeth to piano, cook the dinner and do some homework for your evening class. By the end of the day you are tired because you have had a mentally exacting day, having to juggle and complete so many tasks, and because you have been geographically active, covering a great deal of distance – but mostly in a car or bus. You have barely moved at all.

How active are you really?

An effective way of finding out is by filling in a 24-hour Activity Chart. This chart allows you to record your level of activity by simply colouring each hour according to what you are doing during that time. Once it's completed, you can put your day into perspective and see at a glance whether you are more geographically or mentally active than physically active. You'll also be able to see when you may be able to squeeze in a little more activity. If one day tends to be quite different from the next, you can extend your chart to cover a few days, or perhaps even a whole week. This will give you a fairly good visual indication of how much you move your body over a period of time. Remember, it is the consistency of your actions that reaps the rewards on your weight loss journey.

Count your steps

Some pedometers count calories burned

Some just count steps taken

How do you rate? Once you have filled in your 24-hour Activity Chart and established your average number of steps per day, have a look at the table below, drawn up from research conducted in Japan as a means of classifying activity levels.

Under 5,000 steps a day	'sedentary'
5,000–7,500 steps a day	'low active'
7,500–10,000 steps a day	'somewhat active'
10,000–12,500 steps	'active'
12,500 steps a day +	'highly active'

How much do I have to do?

Between 45 and 90 minutes of moderate-intensity physical activity per day will prevent unhealthy weight gain and keep you within normal BMI range. Sixty minutes is the average recommendation, and should prevent you becoming overweight, or becoming obese if you are already overweight (source: *the International Association for the Study of Obesity*). This 60-minute recommendation is equivalent to a calorie burn of approximately 300 kcal for someone weighing 75kg (165lb) (this is on top of your RMR). A combination of more vigorous, structured exercise and accumulated physical activity can shorten the recommended times and is beneficial for general health.

Please bear in mind that 60 minutes is the average recommendation; it's possible that you may need to be aiming for closer to 90 minutes depending upon your starting-point, your goals and your personal metabolism. Don't feel daunted; this is not impossible. How you achieve it will require some thought and effort, but remember: it is worth it, and you can do it. The results won't be immediate, but with a little consistent effort I promise you will feel better, and feel the difference. You can make the difference.

How can I measure my activity levels?

A good way of finding out how active you are is by wearing some sort of tracking device. The simplest and easiest of these is a pedometer. At the end of each day you can record the number of steps you have accumulated on your 24-hour colour chart. If you don't want to use a pedometer then you can make a note of how much time you spend walking each day. The trouble with this, however, is that it's not very accurate – studies have shown that we tend to overestimate how physically active we are by a whopping 51 per cent!

What is a pedometer?

A great tool, and to my mind an essential item in your weight loss tool kit, a pedometer records the number of steps you take a day. It works by measuring the up-and-down motion of your hip as you walk. It will also measure movements you perform during your day in addition to walking, such as climbing the stairs, gardening or getting in and out of your car. I'd strongly encourage you to invest in a reliable one (see page 240 if you would like to order my own model). As long as you wear your pedometer correctly, it will measure the actual number of steps you take to an accuracy of within 1 per cent. So if you take 100 steps, it should be no more than a step out.

Here's how to wear it. Slide the clip onto your belt or waistband. The most common position is directly above and in line with your knee, but you may have to experiment to find the best place for your shape. If your tummy protrudes over your waistband or belt, it may cause the pedometer to tilt and not work properly. If this is the case try wearing it more to the side of your body.

10,000 steps

Ideally you should aim to achieve 10,000 steps a day (roughly equivalent to a distance of 8km/5 miles). But don't panic if you are not quite there yet; slowly increase your current number of steps by 5–10 per cent each day. If you walk 5,000 steps one day, aim to increase this to between 5,250 and 5,500 the next. Also remember that any improvement at all will get you going in the right direction.

Monitor your progress and you'll feel confident in the knowledge that you are doing what you need to do to widen your Energy Gap and see a change in your body. This will all foster a winning relationship between your body and your brain and reinforce your Template of Success.

Why 10,000?

● Studies have shown that taking 10,000 steps a day without any dietary adjustment can prevent any weight increase, although it may not cause weight loss on its own.

● It also provides a fail-safe foundation for your physical activity and exercise – when life gets busy the first thing that

tends to go is Structured Exercise; by maintaining your 10,000 steps, however, you're still achieving your basic calorie burn.

● Walking is beneficial to your overall health, reducing your risk of developing serious illnesses such as heart disease, some cancers, diabetes and depression. It is also a load-bearing exercise that helps to prevent osteoporosis.

● The 10,000 steps message encourages you not to sit down for too long; if you get up and move every 30 minutes throughout the day, you'll soon clock up those steps.

How many steps have you taken so far today?

Lifestyle and Occupational Activity

As we know, Structured Exercise – sport, or going to the gym, for example – has a major role to play in your overall energy expenditure, and we'll be looking at this in the next chapter. But we also know that it's not the only way to burn off calories. Your body expends energy every time it moves, so your day-to-day activities, whether at work (Occupational Activity) or in your own time (Lifestyle Activity), all contribute to weight loss. Understanding this can inspire everyone to invent ways of incorporating more physical activity into their daily routine.

According to a report published in the *International Journal of Obesity*, people who consistently took short bouts of physical activity ended up expending more calories than those who took longer bouts of Structured Exercise. Remember: your fat cells will not be able to differentiate between a machine at the gym and a flight of stairs at work. The more you move your body, and the more energetically you move it, the greater amount of energy your body will burn and the more weight it will lose.

How can I do it?

Remember: all calories count, independent of the intensity of the activity. If you reduce the time you spend on sedentary things like watching TV, you will free up time for more active pursuits. Small changes such as this, systematically incorporated into your lifestyle, can help widen your Energy Gap. In practical terms you can achieve your target by accumulating more steps throughout your day as well as taking more vigorous Structured Exercise. Here are a couple of ways to help you achieve this, which I've called 'Active Travel' and 'The Workout Wedge'.

Active Travel

This means building more walking into your day-to-day activities. Here are some ideas:

In the workplace

● Stop wearing your mobile phone like a part of your body! Leave it where you will have to get up to answer it.

● When possible avoid emailing colleagues in the building – get up and talk to them. An American study recently reported that using email for 5 minutes out of every hour in your working day could result in a kilo of weight gain every two years – that's potentially 5kg (11lb) of surplus fat by 2014!

● Walk down as well as up the stairs. Apart from accumulating more steps, it's better for you: the impact your body absorbs can help safeguard against osteoporosis.

● Do a chore at lunchtime. Everyone has errands. Be savvy and get something done that involves you moving. Post that letter, pay that cheque in at the bank.

● Piggy-back a habit. Find something you do each day – whether it is buying the newspapers, reading your post or having your morning coffee – and aim to put an additional 1,000 steps on your pedometer before you do it.

At home

● Banish all remote control devices for a week. If you want to change channels or put another CD on, get up and do it!

● If you've got a cordless phone, keep moving while you talk – up and down the stairs if possible.

● Play interval games with the kids! On walks take it in turns with your partner or friend to push the buggy while the other one runs races with the older children; then swap over to catch your breath. The kids will get a great workout too!

● One last thought... Whether at work or at home, use the loo on another floor. The average person goes to the loo five times a day, so you'll be climbing and descending an extra flight of stairs every day.

Walk or cycle whenever you can. Even if you just swap the car for public transport, you'll automatically build more steps in to your day. This is the key to Active Travel.

The Workout Wedge

The idea behind this is that you wedge a workout in between other activities in your day. A Workout Wedge should be at least 2 minutes long, and there's no end to how inventive you can be with it. Here are a couple of ideas.

● Look back at your 24-hour Activity Chart and see where you may be able to wedge in a workout – on your way to work, when you get back home in the evening, in your lunchtime, while the bath is running, or the computer is downloading some software... with a little thought you can be quite creative.

● Try the dinner workout wedge! A number of my clients found this effective, since it targets that time of day when resolve is weak. You get home, you're starving, you're tired, and you can't be bothered to exercise. Wedging in a workout while your dinner is cooking is beneficial in several ways: completing exercise before you eat actually helps you eat less, and leaves you feeling more energized. It really is as simple as prep, exercise and eat! Many dishes take about 20–25 minutes to cook once the preparation's done – there are plenty in the recipe section, for example – and in that time you could...
– Follow a 20-minute exercise video...
– Jog round the block a couple of times...
– Do some stretches, climb some stairs... or try some exercises, such as the Waistband Whittler workout on pages 80–86. It's quick and easy to do!

Navigating the 24

My concept of Navigating the 24 is all about increasing your overall physical activity levels through each and every day, encouraging you to move more, more often, wherever you are. The times when you can be more physically active do add up when you start thinking about it.

Consider this: there are 24 hours in the day and 7 days in the week. That makes 168 hours in each week. Let's say we have the luxury of getting 10 hours' sleep each night (unlikely,

I know – 10 just keeps the arithmetic simple, and maths was never a strong point of mine!). This leaves us (168 – 70 =) 98 hours when we are awake and have the potential to be physically active. Let's suppose we take an hour's structured exercise three times a week, as this is the amount we are generally advised to take and probably the maximum most people think they can squeeze into a busy life. This leaves us with (98 – 3 =) 95 hours when we can move our bodies.

Have a look at the table below and you will soon see how easy this can be.

On an average day, the less active person burns just 30 per cent of the calories the active person uses. If they compensate by going to the gym, they will still use only 60 per cent of the calories burnt by the active person (who does not go to the gym). In addition, the active person keeps their metabolism revved up right through the day. This means they burn an extra 2 calories a minute – which may not sound much, but add that up over 24 hours, 7 days a week, 12 months a year and you soon notch up an extra million calories! That's why you should always opt for the active alternative.

Why the gym is no substitute for an active lifestyle

Less active person	kcals	Active person	kcals	difference
Get someone else to iron while you sit down	34	Iron for 30 minutes	77	43
Get someone else to vacuum while you sit down	11	Vacuum for 10 minutes	40	29
Prepare pre-sliced vegetables	3	Wash, slice and chop your own	28	25
Microwave a ready meal	3	Cook for 30 minutes	67	64
Drive children a half-mile to school	11	Walk children a half-mile to school	56	45
Drive three miles to work	24	Cycle three miles to work	135	111
Use lift to travel up four floors	1	Climb four flights of stairs	11	10
Chat with colleagues for 20 mins at lunchtime	26	Walk and chat for 20 mins at lunchtime	78	52
Shop by internet	17	Walk a mile to the shops and back	311	294
Watch TV for two hours	175	Take a brisk one-hour walk	336	161
Mow the lawn with power mower for 10 mins	50	Use a hand mower for 10 mins	68	18
Read a newspaper for half an hour	34	Play with children for half an hour	94	60
Basic total	389		1301	912
Compensatory gym workout (60 mins)	403	No gym workout	0	-403
Revised total	**792**	**Total**	**1301**	**509**

(Energy expenditure for a 63.5kg/10 stone person. Source: British Heart Foundation health promotion unit, University of Oxford.)

Get a move on!

In a recent study, published in the *American Journal of Clinical Nutrition*, researchers looked at the energy expenditure of women who had lost weight the year before. The single distinguishing feature between those who had successfully kept their weight off and those who had regained the pounds was physical activity. Their energy expenditure was a staggering 44 per cent higher than the women who had regained weight.

Bad week? Not necessarily...

Many people who are trying to lose weight perceive a 'good week' as one when they've got to the gym three times, and a 'bad' week as when they've only managed to attend maybe once or perhaps not at all. (A recent survey revealed the average gym member only shows up once a week!) In fact, if you've been quite physically active in your work and leisure time you may have expended quite a bit of energy without realising it, and have not had a 'bad' week at all.

Try to recognise every small achievement, as it will reinforce your Template of Success. Remember: our success tends to carry over into other behaviour patterns, so it seems easier to make better food choices or decrease portion size. And, of course, the opposite is also true.

Ideally, a 'good week' in *The Weight Loss Bible* journey will include Structured Exercise as well as Occupational and Lifestyle Activity, as you navigate your way through each 24 hours. So even though *The Weight Loss Bible* encourages you to be much more physically active throughout your day, taking time out to do some structured exercise is still important. Exercise intensity improves your fitness and maximises your calorie burn. In addition, you will soon start to experience other benefits, such as increased energy. You'll also sleep better and feel great! This is not just a pleasant side-effect: feeling good about yourself is a vital part of your weight loss journey. It's a wonderful thing, and strengthens your Template of Success. Let's take the next step now.

4get moving

Structured Exercise

So far, we've seen how moving your body can create that all-important Energy Gap – and we've looked at ways in which you can accumulate physical activity in your daily life. With Structured Exercise, however, you have the power to really blast that fat. In fact, it's up to you just how fast you want to travel on your weight loss journey. Basically, the harder you work and the longer you are able to sustain that effort, the more calories you will burn. But don't panic if you are not a natural lover of exercise – as you'll discover, there are lots of fun things to try that don't involve going to the gym. Remember: variety will keep you motivated, and just because you don't like one sort of exercise, it doesn't mean to say that you'll never find anything you enjoy. Ideally, Structured Exercise should combine cardiovascular, resistance and flexibility routines.

Cardiovascular exercise

This is often termed 'endurance' or 'aerobic' (as the large muscles of the body it targets require lots of oxygen to move). It is a good all-round calorie-burner and is usually the most effective method of expending energy in an exercise session.

Cardiovascular exercise should:

- use the large muscles of the body in a continuous, rhythmic fashion;
- be relatively easy to maintain at various workout intensities;
- be enjoyable.

A useful way to optimise energy expenditure in endurance exercise is to vary the intensity. You can do this with forms of exercise that can be easily adjusted or graded to overload the cardio-respiratory system (for instance, increasing the grade of a treadmill or pedalling resistance during stationary cycling). If you're walking or running outdoors, you can increase your pace, and seek out some hills. It's not hard to build periods of intensity into your exercise plans.

Resistance exercise

This causes your muscles to contract to lift a weight. It could be your own body weight, equipment in the gym or even a household object – it doesn't matter, as long as your muscles are made to contract to overcome a force. Resistance exercise tones muscles, and it helps maintain your muscle mass, which can start to decline from your late 20s, so it will make a useful contribution to your long-term weight management.

Building muscle

The main function of resistance exercise in weight loss is to build muscle tissue – one of the most metabolically active kinds of tissue in the body. The more muscle you have, the higher your Resting Metabolic Rate – the calories needed at rest to maintain all of the body's vital processes and systems (see box, page 47). The largest component of the body's total calorie expenditure is the energy needed to maintain its RMR, therefore increasing RMR helps to burn more calories. One study showed a 7 per cent increase in RMR in people aged 56–80 after they completed 12 weeks of resistance training.

Flexibility routines

These involve stretching and moving your joints. Although they tend to be less physically demanding and therefore burn fewer calories, they can be really enjoyable. They can also figure as important components of a warm-up and cool-down. Flexibility work such as yoga and Pilates often proves to be a good introduction to Structured Exercise, especially if you feel you are not a natural exerciser, and the very idea of getting hot and sweaty fills you with inertia!

BODY LAID BARE...

Caution Exercise affects many different body systems. Muscles need a greater supply of energy, so the heart and lungs work faster and more efficiently to keep them well supplied with oxygenated blood. Blood vessels in the intestines, liver, stomach and kidneys narrow so that more blood is directed away from these areas and to the muscles. Regular exercise helps to reduce blood pressure and prevent the build-up of fatty deposits in the arteries, relieves the symptoms of peripheral vascular disease, increases bone density and muscle mass and can help to relieve depression. However, if you have any of the following conditions, you should check with your doctor or specialist before starting an exercise programme.

● If you haven't exercised for some time, or are obese on the BMI scale (see page 30), consult your GP or a fitness instructor. A walking programme would be a good starting point for you.

● If you have coronary heart disease or a history of heart problems, your doctor may refer you for an electrocardiogram (ECG) before you embark on an aerobic exercise programme. This will usually involve you walking, running on a treadmill or cycling an exercise bike while your heart rate is monitored, to see how well you cope with the increased stress.

● If you have had a fracture, dislocation or cartilage injury over the last few years, it is worth seeking advice from a physical therapist or osteopath about the types of exercise that won't put stress on the area in question.

● Anyone with a chronic condition like asthma, osteoarthritis, osteoporosis, high blood pressure or diabetes should follow their GP's advice on the exercise that will be best for them.

In all cases, respect your body. Always start out gradually and don't overdo it. If something hurts, or makes you feel dizzy or short of breath, just stop and seek advice.

What do I need?

You don't have to spend a fortune on exercise kit and special equipment, but there are a few items that can make the whole exercise experience a lot more enjoyable. You might want to consider the following:

● **A cap with a peak** – keeps both rain and low sunlight off your face and out of your eyes.

● **A warm hat** – You can lose up to 60 per cent of your body heat through your head, so in winter a warm hat can be a smart investment. It will also keep long hair under control on a windy day, but make sure it won't blow off.

● **Gloves** – In cold weather your extremities can get pretty chilly. Invest in a pair of gloves with some grip so you can wear them on a bike or while pushing a buggy. Many sports varieties are made using breatheable, comfortable and functional materials – find them at sports shops.

● **A lightweight waterproof** – important to keep you dry in spring showers or autumn downpours. For convenience, get one that can roll up quite small.

● **Heavier waterproofs** – good for the wettest weather. I actually use golf waterproofs and have found them to be both functional and attractive.

● **Breatheable tops** – a long-sleeved one for cooler weather and a sleevless one or a T-shirt for when it's warmer.

● **Legwear** – invest in something with some stretch. Lycra does not have to be that horrifically ugly, sweat-pant style which originally flooded the market a few years back – there are many stylish leggings available. Shorter legwear – calf, knee or thigh length – is more comfortable in warm weather. Ultimately go for whatever you feel most comfortable in.

● **Cycling shorts** – buy these if you are intending to do quite a bit of cycling – personally, I think they are worth it.

● **Sunglasses** – Yes, you can still exercise with style. Even when it's not that bright, wearing clear lenses will keep grit and pollution out of your eyes.

Trainers:

Shoes are crucial. You don't have to spend a fortune, but getting a good, well-fitting pair is money well spent. Be aware that an old shoe may look in good condition when its supportive qualities have diminished considerably with wear. When buying trainers, bear the following in mind:

● Shop for shoes in the afternoon, because feet tend to swell during the day.
● Athletic shoes should be comfortable from the start, requiring minimal breaking-in.
● When trying on shoes, try them out on both carpet and hard surfaces, simulating an outdoor walking or running experience in the shop.

● Before you part with your cash, run through this checklist: FIT, COMFORT, CUSHIONING and CONTROL. Don't buy trainers, no matter how much you like the look of them, unless they provide all four of these qualities.
● Replace your athletic shoes every 300 to 500 miles (or 4–6 months). Your feet may carry you as far as 12,000 miles in your lifetime – so take care of them.

Remember this:

Cushioning – protects the foot from injury
Flexibility – transmits the power of your body efficiently
Stability – controls the motion of the foot and ankle
(so you don't get sprains, strains or even fractures).

How hard do I have to work?

With Lifestyle and Occupational Exercise, consistency's the key. However, with Structured Exercise it's how hard you are working that truly counts. It's here that you can develop your fitness and build up the amount of energy you burn. But what is most important is working at the right intensity for your safety, enjoyment and success. I therefore strongly advise monitoring of some sort; if nothing else, it will strengthen your brain/body relationship and reinforce your all-important Template of Success.

How to monitor intensity

Some methods are simpler than others, but it's vital to choose at least one. Exercising too hard will not be enjoyable, and will increase your likelihood of giving up as well as your risk of injury; not exercising hard enough will not yield results. When taking Structured Exercise, make sure you can:

● Hold a conversation with a friend. This means that you should be able to have a breathy conversation with them – not talk to them continuously.
● Increase your washing load! At the end of your structured exercise session you should need to put your exercise kit in the washing machine.
● Happily strip off! You should feel warm enough to take off a layer of clothing. Depending on the time of year, this could be a sweatshirt, long-sleeved T-shirt or tracksuit.
● Do a little more. At the end of your structured exercise session you should certainly feel as if you have exerted yourself, but you should also feel refreshed – and although you have been physically active you should feel as if you could do a little more if you really had to.
● You should not feel as if you are ready to collapse, or feel dizzy or queasy. If you do, you have worked too hard.
● The chart opposite rates the intensity of exertion on a scale of 1 to 10. In a Structured Exercise session, you should be working to a perceived exertion rate of between 5 and 8.

Heart-rate monitoring

Heart rate increases in proportion to exercise intensity, so recording heart rate is a fairly accurate measure. Heart-rate monitoring can be done manually, or by using a piece of equipment such as a heart-rate monitor watch. These use electrodes mounted on a sealed electronic transmitter that is attached to the chest with an elastic belt. They pick up the heart's electrical impulses and relay them to a wrist monitor that displays them as beats per minute. Most heart-rate monitors give you an immediate reading, and some models allow you to set training limits, effectively acting as your own little personal trainer.

To monitor your heart rate manually, you can record your pulse either at your wrist or at your carotid artery. This can be found at the side of the neck; extend your chin away from your shoulders and with your first and second finger apply a small amount of pressure on either side of your windpipe. You should feel a small pulse underneath your fingers.

A heart-rate training zone is between 50 and 85 per cent of your maximum heart rate. If you are new to exercising, you should start off at the lower end of this range and gradually work upwards. To calculate your maximum heart rate, use the following equation:
For men: 220 minus age
For women: 228 minus age.
From here, you can work out your own specific training zone by calculating 50 and 85 per cent of your personal maximum heart rate. Please note that as your cardiovascular fitness improves, your heart rate response will be lower for the same absolute exercise intensity. This means that you will have to work at a higher intensity to achieve the same energy burn in the same amount of time.

If all these calculations seem a little daunting, don't fret – there's a much simpler way, described in the chart opposite, which many of my clients prefer.

Perceived Rate of Exertion

Rating	Perceived Exertion	Examples of Exertion	Clothing/Sweat Factor	Chat Factor
0	Nothing at all	Lying completely still in bed, sleeping	Warm clothes or covers required as body is still and not generating heat. No sweat.	Can sleep-talk to your heart's content!
1	Very, very weak	Watching TV or a film in the cinema, sitting in a boring meeting at work, sewing, or reading a book.	Layer of clothes dependent on temperature of environment. No sweat.	Can chat to your heart's content
2	Weak	Browsing in the shops, playing the piano, typing on your laptop, eating dinner, sitting and chatting with friends, filling dishwasher.	Layer of clothes dependent on temperature of environment. No sweat.	Can chat to heart's content.
3	Moderate	Walking the dog, walking to work, playing a leisurely game of doubles tennis.	Feel a little warm in the clothes you are wearing. Starting to sweat.	Able to talk comfortably.
4	Somewhat strong	Climbing escalators, carrying the shopping up several flights of stairs, cycling for pleasure.	Feel like you need to take off an item of clothing and tie it around your waist. Starting to perspire on your body and face.	Able to talk but not sing.
5	Stronger	Manually mowing your lawn, walking very briskly.	Need to take off a layer of clothes to avoid sweating.	Able to hold a breathy conversation.
6	Harder	Walking briskly up a hill, or walking very very fast, pushing a pram up a slope, digging in the garden, lightly jogging.	Perspiration felt on body and face.	Able to hold a conversation but it's something of a struggle... uncomfortable.
7	Strong	Fast jogging or running, lifting heavy objects such as furniture or weights in the gym. Can only continue for a limited time.	Appropriate clothing worn to allow body to breathe. Definite sweating on face and body.	Able to hold a sporadic conversation with short pauses for breath.
8	Very Strong	Running fast to catch the last bus home, skipping with a rope, circuit training. Have to force yourself.	Body feeling very warm. Sweating. Light clothing worn to allow movement.	Unable to hold a continual conversation (you're mostly monosyllabic).
9	Very, very hard	Running in a race.	Body feels very hot. Sweating during and immediately after activity.	Unable to hold a conversation.
10	Maximum effort. You can work no harder.	Running for your life.	Your whole body and head feel very hot.	Unable to speak.

Getting fitter on your weight loss journey

As you get fitter, you will find that the exercises you started with become easier.

● Make your Structured Exercise sessions longer
● Gradually increase your exercise intensity in small increments. Boosting your effort by 5–10 per cent is a good way to progress.
● Exercising using different of pieces of equipment in a gym can be challenging, as different muscle groups are involved.
● Introduce interval training.

Interval training

Interval training combines periods of high-intensity work with moderate- to light-intensity work. It is highly effective, and can be a useful form of exercise to complement an active lifestyle, helping you improve your fitness as well as aid weight management. Design your interval-training programme according to how fit you are, how long you plan to exercise and what your specific aims are. You are the one in control: you select the form of exercise you wish to do, you apply the intensity and you are away.

Here is a sample interval-training programme, intended to enhance the body's calorie-burning capacity.

Always start gradually with a 3–5 minute warm-up of light-intensity cardiovascular exercise to prepare the lungs, heart and muscles for the workout to follow. Try steady walking, rolling the shoulders and circling the arms.

Train for 4 minutes at a high intensity followed by 4 minutes at a moderate to light intensity. Try brisk walking interspersed with more moderate walking.

Alternate these 4-minute intervals for the entire workout. During the high-intensity interval, you should feel 'comfortably challenged' (a PRE of 7–8) . During the moderate-intensity interval you should feel 'somewhat challenged' (a PRE of 5–6).

Start off with a 20-minute workout and gradually progress up to 60 minutes over several weeks. Your rate of progress will depend on your fitness.

To get fitter and keep burning calories you need to exercise to a point of 'overload'. This is when your body feels physically challenged. As long as you can hear your body saying to you 'Oh, that feels a bit harder – what's going on here?', you can be sure that you have provided 'overload'.

Measuring your fitness progress

Just as you're keeping track of the changes in your body shape and weight, it's also useful – and very gratifying – to see how fit you're becoming. There's a variety of ways to do this, but one of the simplest and easiest is with a timed walk of a set distance. It could be a kilometre or a mile, or a favourite route, but it has to be somewhere you can return regularly without a problem. Note down your heart rate when you start, when you finish, and then again a minute later, as well as the time it takes to complete your route. As you get

fitter your heart muscle becomes stronger and is able to pump the oxygenated blood your body requires more efficiently. Over a period of time you should expect to see not only a faster walking time but a drop in your heart rate as well. Try to test your fitness every four weeks.

Start heart rate This is your resting heart rate, taken immediately before your walk. Find your pulse (either wrist or neck will do), record your HR for 10 seconds and multiply it by six.

Finish heart rate This is your heart rate immediately after your walk. Find your pulse and record your HR for a full 60 seconds (it will start to slow down during this time).

Recovery heart rate After you have recorded your finish HR, wait one minute and then record your HR for a further 60 seconds. This will give you the greatest indication of how your fitness has improved over the 28 days. The faster your heart returns to its normal rate the more efficient it is.

Date	Time to complete	Start HR	Finish HR	Recovery HR:
18/3	10 mins	23	23	23
19/3	15 mins	25	22	20
20/3	20 mins	24	26	18
21/3	20 mins	24	22	18

Injury prevention

As you become increasingly active, you may come up against a few niggling aches and pains in various parts of your body. This is to be expected if you are new to exercise and in particular if you have begun to walk a lot more. Many of these can be be easily minimised with a little know-how. Try these tips, which will help you walk stronger, longer and burn more energy at the same time.

Avoid shin pain

Foot roll: Standing with your feet almost together, roll up onto your toes, hold for 2 seconds and roll back down. Then roll onto the outside of your feet, hold for 2 seconds and roll back down. Next roll onto your heels with the toes off the ground, hold for 2 seconds and roll back down. Repeat this sequence 10 times before every walk.

Avoid knee pain

Straight leg raise: Sit on the ground with your legs extended in front of you. Bend your right leg and place your right foot flat on the ground. Rest your hands behind you and sit up straight. With your left foot flexed, contract your left thigh and raise your leg 15–30cm (6–12 inches) off the floor. Hold for 5 seconds and then lower. Do 10 lifts, and then switch sides. Perform the sequence 2–4 times a week.

Avoid aching legs

Hip and calf stretch: Stand with your feet together, then step your right foot about 3–4 foot lengths in front of you. Both feet should be pointing forward. Bend your right knee so it is just above but not in front of your right foot. Check both big toes are facing forward. Keep your left leg straight and your left heel on the ground to feel a stretch in your left calf. Flatten your lower back and tuck in your pelvis so you also feel a stretch in the front of your hip. Hold for 4–7 slow deep breaths, release, and repeat on the other side. Stretch each leg twice after each walk.

Lower calf stretch: Stand close to a tree or lamppost and rest the ball of your right foot on the trunk or post so that your heel is still on the ground. Bend your right knee in towards the post; you should feel a stretch in the lower part of the calf. Hold for 10–15 seconds and repeat twice each side. Do this at the end of each walk.

Avoid upper arm tension

Upper body stretch: Stand with your feet about shoulder-distance apart and raise your right arm over your head, bending your elbow so your right hand is behind your head. Place your left hand on your right elbow and gently pull your elbow to the left, allowing your upper body to bend slightly to the left. Hold for 4–7 deep breaths, release and repeat on the other side. Stretch each side twice after every walk.

Tips for top technique

How you perform your exercises will not only affect your rate of progress but also your risk of injury. The following simple tips will help you build a fit, strong body and achieve better results in less time:

The mistake: Rolling the knee inwards so it is not aligned with the toes when you are performing lunges, step aerobics or pliés. This can injure the knees.

Put it right: Keep knee and toes in line. Make sure as you look down you can see your toes. Imagine drawing a line down the front of your knee cap – if you extend it all the way down, it should be in line with your second toe.

The mistake: Leading with the chin in abdominal exercises in an effort to curl the upper body off the floor. This puts strain on the neck and lessens the effectiveness of the exercise, because you are using your neck and shoulder muscles instead of your abdominals.

Put it right: Lift from the breast bone. Imagine the movement starts from the breast bone. Keep the chin and neck in line by imagining that your ear lobes and collarbone are always in alignment.

A time for you

One in four of us experiences depression at some point in our lives, and regular physical activity is one of the best depression busters around. I'm also a great believer that Structured Exercise is a time for you. We live in a fast-paced world, but Structured Exercise gives you little moments of 'me' time. It's an investment in yourself that no one can afford not to make.

The mistake: The walking stomp! As you increase your walking speed, technique can be compromised and the foot tends to land heavily rather than in a controlled way.

Put it right: Keep your upper body lifted as you walk, imagining you have a cup of water balanced on each shoulder that you mustn't spill. Focus on walking through the whole foot as you land as well.

The mistake: Slumping as you step up. Often when you step up onto a bench or even the stairs your body remains slumped and the legs, back and hips never fully extend. This puts pressure on your spine, hinders posture and may contribute to injury.

Put it right: Make sure you extend upwards fully each time you take a step. Keep your head high and be proud of the space your body occupies.

So... you've done your homework and you've learned a lot. Now it's time to have fun. You'll soon see from the list on the following pages that cardiovascular exercise is not all about treadmills and stationary cycling!

Choose your cardio exercises

The world is your oyster! You can opt for intrepid sports like white-water rafting or Himalayan climbing, or activities that fit in with your lifestyle, such as skipping with your children in the back garden or cycling to work. The following list includes some obvious and some less common suggestions, with advice on how to perform them and what they will do for you (as well as the calories you can burn).

Walking

Walking is the simplest, most accessible and least expensive form of exercise, and it works for the vast majority of people. As well as burning calories, it streamlines your hips and thighs. To make walking an effective form of structured exercise,

however, you need to establish your optimum walking pace. First of all, get yourself somewhere where there is plenty of room – a park, country path, open land or quiet pavement. Start walking and gradually pick up your speed – swinging your arms faster will help. Continue to increase your pace, making sure you maintain a walking stride until you feel yourself involuntarily breaking into a jog. This is known as your break point. From this point drop back to your walking pace (a small deceleration – maybe 3–5 per cent), and you now have your optimum walking pace. You should feel like you are walking with a purpose, and much faster than you normally would. On your first few outings I suggest you do this break point drill several times to help you become familiar with your optimum pace.

There are a few postural hints you should bear in mind when it comes to perfecting your walking technique:

- Strike the ground with the heel first, rolling through the foot then pushing off with the toe.
- Think 'tall' – don't slump into your hips.
- Pull in your abdominal muscles to support your back.
- Relax your shoulders and let your arms swing naturally by your sides without crossing your body.
- Use your natural stride – don't try to lengthen it. If you want to increase your pace, try moving your arms faster – your legs will naturally speed up.
- Wear properly cushioned trainers that fit you snugly but without pinching.

Belly-dancing

What you do: When you think belly-dancing, you may think Middle-Eastern restaurants. Don't. There are now any number of classes around the country providing tuition in more cultured styles. Egyptian belly-dancing is more classical and skilful, while the Turkish style tends to be more overtly sexy!

Great for: Boosting your self-esteem in a non-competitive environment, getting your heart bumping and increasing your body awareness – as well as teaching you a few extra little moves to show off on the dance floor or the bedroom! The

waist and midriff will become more toned and shapely, and you should also find you get better mobility in your spine.

How much you burn: Up to 140 calories in 30 minutes.

Swimming

What you do: Since the water provides a certain degree of support, energy expenditure can be quite low but get competent at swimming and you can make swimming part of your regular aerobic exercise together with more weight-supporting workouts. Aqua classes can be fun and also provide toning benefits due to the resistance of the water.

Great for: Swimming involves the whole body and is fantastic if you suffer from joint problems as the water can provide support to limbs especially if you're arthritic.

How much you burn: Up to 190 calories in 30 minutes.

Salsa aerobics

What you do: A South American dance brought into the studio. It's just what you need if you want to exercise but don't want to feel like you're working out.

Great for: Strengthening your heart and your lungs. Targets the often-neglected oblique muscles that help trim and define your waist.

How much you burn: Up to 150 calories in 30 minutes.

BodyJam

What you do: Bodyjam incorporates a variety of dance techniques that are simple and easy to follow.

Great for: Developing a sense of achievement as you master dance routines while your heart and lungs get a good cardiovascular workout at the same time. It'll also tone your thighs and bottom, and the arm movements will help with your overall co-ordination.

How much you burn: Up to 180 calories in 30 minutes.

Iceskating

What you do: Grab some friends and head down to the local ice rink. It's great fun!

Great for: Your balance – and once the basic moves are mastered, you'll benefit from a firmer bottom, streamlined legs, greater poise and better posture. You'll also get a great workout just from getting up every time you fall over!

How much you burn: Up to 234 calories in 30 minutes.

Jogging

What you do: Either indoors on a treadmill or outdoors in the fresh air, jogging or running is an excellent all-round aerobic exercise. Make sure you have good supportive shoes and when starting out alternate brisk walking with jogging. Try 30 seconds' jogging to 60 seconds' walking and gradually reduce the ratio of walking to jogging until you can jog continuously for 20 minutes.

Great for: Improving the stamina of your heart and lungs. It's a good energy burner as you are having to support the whole of your body as you move.

How much you burn: Up to 300 calories in 30 minutes.

Tennis

What you do: Tennis as a calorie burner can be a little deceptive. Vigorous energetic games of tennis can be great fun and a wonderful excuse to get outside, but do be aware that the stop-start nature of the game and the social nature of this great sport can mean you burn fewer calories than you might think.

Great for: Toning arms and legs, as well as a cardio workout if you run for those wide balls.

How much you burn: depends on intensity of game.

Ball sports

What you do: Whether it's basketball, netball, rounders or football, ball sports are great fun and you don't always need to put together a team to enjoy messing around with a ball.

Great for: Hand-eye co-ordination and cardio fitness. The social element of these activities can be a great motivator to keep you exercising so combine them with healthy picnics in the park on Sundays and get a whole group of you playing.

How much you burn: depends on the sport and your position in the team (for example, goalkeepers won't burn so many calories as midfielders).

Rock-climbing

What you do: Many large leisure centres and outdoor pur-suits centres have specially designed climbing walls. If you want to be at one with nature, specialist courses can take you to stunning locations such as the Dolomites in Italy, the Brecon Beacons in Wales, or the Cairngorms in Scotland.

Great for: All-round muscle strength and tone. The step-up action is especially good for toning buttocks and thighs and the whole body co-ordination challenges mind and body.

How much you burn: depends how challenging the climb is.

Circus training

What you do: There are a number of circus schools and courses up and down the country. Some holiday companies now offer circus skills classes as part of their activities pro-gramme. If you have ever been to a circus and thought 'I would love to try that' — then here's your chance.

Great for: Improving overall body awareness, self-esteem and body confidence. Dependent on the circus skills you choose, you can improve your upper and or lower body, tone and improve agility and flexibility.

Thai boxing

What you do: A form of martial arts using bare hands. Lessons are widely available in gyms and martial arts centres. It originated in medieval times when arms, legs, elbows and

knees were all used as weapons in close fighting. Nowadays the ancient spiritual connections are still maintained and are embedded in the rules of the sport.

Great for: Building strength through agility and cardio fitness. It is a great form of self-defence as well being good for boosting confidence and self-esteem.

Golf

What you do: Walk the golf course and you will be clocking up significant steps on your pedometer.

Great for: The rotational nature of the golf swing can be great for a toned torso but do start out slowly — remember the Tiger Woods and Nick Faldos of this world spend hours training to help create a balanced smooth swing.

How much you burn: Up to 130 calories in 30 minutes.

Horse-riding

What you do: The horse may appear to be doing all the hard work – but in reality you're getting a good lower-body toning session, plus a healthy dose of fresh air. It is less cardiovascular than other activities, however.

Great for: Calming you, and stimulating the release of feel-good brain waves. Your inner thighs and lower abdominal muscles benefit from horse-riding, and you have to focus on having good posture to ensure you stay on your horse!

How much you burn: Up to 120 calories in 30 minutes.

Kite-flying

What you do: Getting outdoors in pursuit of the most simple and innocent of childhood pastimes can be great fun. Take it in turns with your partner to run after the kite, collect it and set it up for its next flight.

Great for: Blowing away the cobwebs if you have been stuck indoors all week (remember: daylight raises your levels of Vitamin D). Boost your cardiovascular and calorie-burning efforts by finding yourself a hill, and taking it in turns to run up and down it to fetch the kite. Your hips, thighs and bottom will all benefit.

How much you burn: Up to 135 calories in 30 minutes.

Cycling

What you do: Use your bike to run errands, or cycle to school with the kids – it's a fantastic way for exercise to creep into your day. You'll be surprised how on shorter journeys you can often get to your chosen destination quicker than by car.

Great for: All-round cardiovascular exercise that's especially great if you've got children. Since body weight is supported, and the pressure applied to the pedal is relative to the weight of the cyclist, both adults and children can cycle together quite easily, without the child feeling exhausted before Mum and Dad! Follow cycle routes around places of interest or discover great pubs out in the country. If you're mountain biking your thighs, arms and upper back will gain definition, while more level cycling can be a significant calorie burner.

How much you burn: Up to 240 calories in 30 minutes.

Skipping

What you do: Skip either by jumping with feet together (harder) or with a running motion (easier and less jarring on joints). This is intense – start with 20-second bouts and build up to 5 minutes' continuous skipping. Check that as you land your heels come down and your knees are soft.

Great for: Increasing the stamina of your heart and lungs. A fantastic energy burner.

How much you burn: Up to 280 calories in 30 minutes.

Downhill skiing

What you do: Swoosh down the slopes! Preferably on skis and not your backside. Totally exhilarating, it is enough to give any fitness cynic a massive adrenaline high.

Great for: Working the legs and abdominal muscles. Using your poles to help you get up small inclines will target your arms, too.

How much you burn: A cool 374 calories an hour.

Snowboarding

What you do: It's akin to surfing on snow, as you stand sideways on a board. Snowboard teachers claim a novice of any age can be gliding down slopes competently within a few days. You never know – you may even be overtaking the kids!

Great for: Your legs and buttocks; it also tones your waist and abdominals.

How much you burn: This full-body blast burns about 400 calories an hour.

Snowshoeing

What you do: Snowshoeing is just walking in the snow but with special footwear. It is fast becoming the latest fashionable alpine sport, and many resorts have specially marked out scenic routes for enthusiasts.

Great for: Giving your thighs and buttocks a great workout.

How much you burn: With snow as your natural resistance, even walking at a moderate pace on flat terrain can burn as many as 500 calories an hour – more than either skiing or snowboarding will do.

Resistance and flexibility exercises

These can often be a useful entry point into more structured exercise sessions, since they require less physical effort. As with cardio, there's a huge range you can choose from. Here's just a small selection.

Pilates

Pilates involves deep muscle training according to the principles of German fitness instructor Joseph Pilates. Pilates helps you to develop a strong 'core' (body centre), consisting of the deep abdominal muscles along with the muscles closest to the spine, thus protecting the spine and keeping the pelvis correctly aligned. You will be shown matwork exercises that you can perform yourself, at home, and reformer exercises that need to be performed on a piece of studio equipment called a reformer (*see above*). Pilates can be good for creating a toned and sleek body without bulk, and an excellent form of exercise for improving your posture and helping to correct muscle alignment, but it has little cardiovascular value.

Yoga

Broadly speaking, there are three styles of yoga – Hatha, Astanga and Iyengar. They differ in many ways, one of which is how much they demand of you physically. For best toning effects, opt for Astanga (or Vinyasa, which is not so well known). This incorporates more postures that are supported by body weight, and you often move from one posture to another by supporting part of your weight with your arms. Iyengar and Hatha styles are usually more gentle, and while breathing techniques are an integral part of all yoga practice, you tend to find there is more emphasis on breathing and relaxation in these two styles.

Weight training

Weight training involves the use of hand-held weights or weight machines to strengthen specific muscle groups of the body (the vast majority of health clubs will have weight-training facilities). Following a progressive weight-training programme can enhance muscle mass – but it can also make you heavier. Don't worry, however – muscle weighs more than fat, and providing you are mindful of your diet as well as your exercise regime, you will feel your clothes getting loser as your size decreases. Use weight training to complement your cardiovascular exercise, creating tone and shape in your body as you shed the fat. This means lifting lighter weights but with more repetitions, thus enhancing the cardiovascular benefits of the workout. In the Action Plans in Chapter 6 you'll see how I incorporate resistance training to augment your cardiovascular gains and increase your energy expenditure.

Toning classes

These classes focus on resistance exercises that use your own body weight, small weights, resistance bands or balls to tone your body. Their focus will vary from class to class, but generally the idea is to increase tone with more repetitions and lighter weights.

Targeting Workouts

We all have parts of our body that pose particular problems and seem to be immune to all our weight-loss efforts. This is where these Targeting Workouts come in. You can do them on your own, or use a couple of your favourite exercises as Workout Wedges or as intervals in your cardiovascular routines. First of all, let's spend a little time looking at technique, since if it's flat abs you want, it's not quantity but quality that counts. These simple flat tummy skills will help you to get great results in no time.

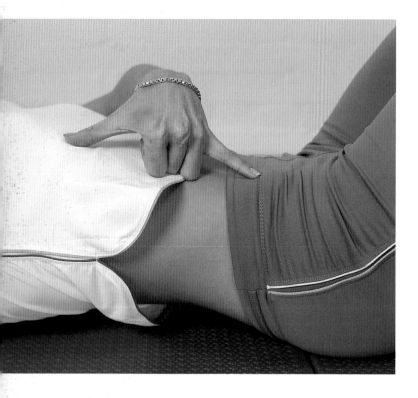

The rib-hip connection

What it does: Gives you an instant smaller trimmer waistline.

Lie on the floor with your knees bent and place your hands around your rib cage, fingertips facing in towards your breast bone. As you take a deep breath in, feel your rib cage expand. This is how most people start their tummy exercises. **STOP!!** By doing this you will get a bigger waist!

To combat this, as you breathe out imagine you are wearing a corset that needs to be tightened up. As you pull your stomach down you will have engaged your internal oblique muscles, which will help you regain a 'pinched-in' waist. Try to feel relaxed and comfortable in this position.

Another method to try is to place your thumb on your lower ribs and your little finger on the top of your hip bone and draw these two points together with a small contraction of the abdominal muscles. Your spine should be in a neutral position, with a small space between the floor and your lower back. This neutral position will vary from person to person, dependent upon the shape of your spine.

Engage the rib-hip connection and neutral spine before doing any abdominal exercise.

Lift and lengthen

What it does: Gives you lean, flat abdominals.

1 Lie on the floor with your knees bent and with the rib-hip connection engaged. Start to SLOWLY lift your upper body off the floor leading with the breastbone (not the head, chin or nose).

2 Lengthen through the crown of the head as you lift and then lower again. To help you, imagine your head has to touch the edge of a semi-circle throughout the whole movement. The movement should feel long, as you lift up and down.

Stable jelly belly

What it does: Stops troublesome lower tummy bulges and supports your back, preventing back pain.

1 To really flatten that lower jelly belly, you need to target the deep transverse abdominal muscle (the one you are contracting when you lie on the floor to do up your jeans). To help you do this, kneel on all fours and pull your belly button up to the spine and towards the ceiling as far as possible. Test how good you are at this by getting a friend or the kids to try to push your tummy a little – it should feel stable and shouldn't move.

2 Now repeat, with your tummy muscles relaxed; when someone pushes you this time, you'll notice that you wobble and have no stability.

Waistband Whittler

The first of our Targeting Workouts, for toning those abs

Breast bone lift

What it does: Trims the upper waist and tummy area.

1 Lie on the floor face up, knees slightly bent and feet on the floor but far enough away from your bottom so that you feel as if your toes are just about to lift up. Place your hands at the side of your head and raise your head slightly off the floor. This is your start position.

Top tip: This is a very subtle exercise. Make sure your keep your abdominals pulled in throughout. You shouldn't feel any strain in your neck, thighs or lower back.

2 From here, lift no more than 5cm, leading from the breast bone. Hold this small lift for 4 counts and lower back to the start position. Lower your head to the floor.

3 To make it harder: start with one leg extended while the other remains bent and repeat the Breast bone lift. Hold for 4 counts then lower and repeat with the other leg extended.

Dead bug

What it does: A great total tummy toner without any neck pain.

1 *Start position:* Lie on your back and lift your legs and arms off the floor, so that your knees are bent just above your hips and your arms are directly over your shoulders, palms facing forwards. Keeping as still as possible, firmly pull your abdominals back into your spine. Hold this position for 2 sets of 8 counts.

Top tip: Make sure your legs are not too close in to your body, otherwise this becomes too easy. Experiment holding your knees a little further away so you feel some tension in your abdominals.

2 Lower your right foot down to the floor and tap with your heel 4 times, without letting your lower back arch.

3 Still contracting your abdominals, raise the right foot back up then lower your left foot to tap your heel on the floor.

4 *To make it harder:* Start in the dead bug position. Slowly lower the right leg and right arm towards the floor at the same time. The distance between arm and knee should stay the same – imagine you're holding a beach ball between them.

5 Gently 'kiss' the floor with your heel then slowly lift the arm and leg back up to the dead bug position. Repeat with the left arm and the left leg, keeping your abdominals firmly pulled down throughout.

Belt pulls

What it does: Flattens and improves the postural support of your abdominals.

1 *Start position*: First put on a belt that will buckle up snugly around your waist. Kneel on all fours with your hands under your shoulders and your knees under your hips. Start with your abdominals relaxed and, keeping your back straight, firmly draw in your abdominal muscles so you create space between your tummy and your belt. You should be able to slip your fingers in between your belt and your tummy. Hold this position for 30 seconds, breathing smoothly throughout. Relax for 10 seconds. Repeat 5 times.

2 *To make it harder:* Keep your back straight as you extend your left arm and right leg. Now draw in your abdominal muscles firmly to create the space between your belt and your tummy. Repeat with the right arm and left leg.

3 Draw your right elbow and left knee together so that they just touch. Hold for 4 counts, then extend out again. Repeat 3 times, and then draw your left elbow and right knee together and repeat 3 times.

Ab reach

What it does: Firms and flattens the whole of the abdominal area.

1 *Start position*: Lie on your back with your knees slightly bent and your feet positioned so that your toes are raised a little off the floor. Lift your upper body, leading from your breast-bone, and place your hands on your thighs.

2 Lift about 5cm from the breast bone, trying to reach further down your thighs with your hands if you can, then lower back to your start position and extend your arms above your head, keeping your shoulders off the floor.

Top tip: Positioning your feet slightly further away from your bottom ensures that your spine is kept long along the floor, helping to engage and target the troublesome lower tummy area.

Oblique rib-to-hip lift

What it does: Targets the waist.

1 *Start Position:* Lie on your back with your knees bent and feet extended away from your bottom. Stretch your right arm out to the side, and touch the fingers of your left hand to the side of your head. Lift your upper body from the ground.

2 Pull your stomach to the floor and stretch across as if you are trying to fold your left shoulder towards your right hip bone. Repeat 8 times, then do the same in the opposite direction, lifting your right shoulder towards your left hip bone.

Tips to prevent neck pain

When the abdominal muscles are not strong enough to support the weight of your torso as you lift, discomfort in the neck can result. This discomfort should lessen as your abdominal muscles get stronger and firmer, so do stick with your Waistband Whittler exercises. In the meantime, however, here are a few tips to minimise neck strain.

Solution one: Place a towel underneath your shoulders and hold onto the corners, pulling tight to cradle your head and neck as you lift. Avoid yanking your head up with your hands as you lift. Remember: always lift from your breast bone and not from your chin.

Solution two: Place a rolled towel at the nape of your neck and hold tightly at both ends as you lift and lower. Also, strange as it sounds, press your tongue firmly against the roof of your mouth as you lift and lower. This appears to stabilise the neck muscles, giving support to your head.

Lower tummy muscles 'popping out'

Sometimes as we lift, the lower abdominal muscles can 'pop' out, making the lower back unstable. Here are a couple of solutions to help train the abdominal wall to flatten.

Solution one Check you have the rib-hip connection (see page 76) then place a ruler across your lower abdominal muscles. As you lift, try to keep the ruler in place by focusing on drawing down through the lower abdominal wall.

Solution two Wear a belt for your abdominal exercises. Buckle it so you have room for a little movement between your abdominals and the belt. As you lift, focus on keeping your abdominals away from the belt buckle and not pressing against it.

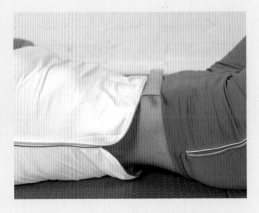

Exercises for specific body shapes

On page 34, you assessed whether your body shape is like a pear, an apple, a carrot or a red pepper. Now I'm going

to show you some exercises for each shape that will help you firm up your assets and downsize the problem areas.

Pear-shaped

You want to: streamline hips and thighs; create a visual balance between upper and lower body

Action Emphasis on slimming the lower body while creating shape and definition in the upper body will benefit general health as well as promoting the optimum body shape change.

Target Try to do these exercises 4 times a week.

1 Can opener and extension

What it does: Streamlines outer hips and thighs and helps to lengthen and tone muscles of whole leg.
How many you do: 12–16 slow repetitions on each side.

1 Lie on your side, with your knees bent as if sitting on a chair. Keeping your feet and knees together lift your feet off the floor. This is your start position.

2 Keeping the feet together use your outer thigh muscles to open the top knee as wide as possible then extend the leg out to full length. Bring the leg back into the bent leg position and repeat. Turn onto the other side and repeat.

2 Frontal raise and lateral arm combo

What it does: Gives shape and tone to the front of arm as well as creating and defining the shoulders.

How many you do: 4 counts up, 4 counts out, 8 counts down, all repeated 4 times.

1 Stand straight with good posture, holding weights (or water bottles) in each hand, with your palms facing away from your thighs.

2 Lift the weights slowly to eye level, to the count of 4, keeping your elbows in line with your wrists.

3 Extend your arms out to the sides, level with your shoulders, for 4 counts and lower to the start position again on 8 counts. Repeat.

3 All fours cross leg combo

What it does: Targets the outer buttock area as well as lifting and firming the main buttock cheeks.

How many you do: 16 repetitions with each leg

1 Start by kneeling on all fours, then lower your forehead to rest on your hands, which should be in loose fists. Lift up one knee, with the sole of the foot towards the ceiling.

2 Keeping your hips level, lower the knee to the outside of the opposite calf. Lift the leg back to original position. Repeat with the other leg.

Cardio

Swimming can be a great all-over cardiovascular form of exercise, stimulating your heart and lungs. Breast stroke and front crawl are particularly beneficial for those with pear shapes as the strokes engage all the back muscles, helping to give tone, shape and definition. Regular swimming for 30 minutes 4 times a week will develop more shape in your deltoid shoulder muscles as well as improving your cardiovascular stamina.

Carrot-shaped

You want to: create a nipped defined waist.

Action There are two sets of oblique muscles which help form a trim waist; training both of these effectively will create that smaller firmer midriff. The rib cage is often expanded through stress or pregnancy, giving your torso a wider appearance. Master the rib-hip connection (see page 76) before you do any of these exercises and you will really notice a difference.

Target Your body will benefit from doing these exercises 5 times a week.

1 Towel oblique lift

What it does: Helps lengthen and tighten a short thick waist.
How many you do: This is challenging, so build up gradually to 10 each side.

1 Lie on your side with a rolled-up towel under your waist. Make sure your top hip bone is directly over the lower hip bone. Extend one arm under your head, straighten your legs and pull in your tummy muscles to give support. Rest your top arm on the floor in front of you.

2 Using your waist muscles gently lift your body upwards. Try to avoid using the top hand to push you up – just use it to keep your balance. Lower your body again in a controlled manner. Do the set number of repetitions then turn onto the other side and repeat.

2 Water bottle lift

What it does: Defines and trims waist as it flattens lower abdominals.

How many you do: Perform the whole sequence 3 times.

1 Lie on your back with your knees bent and establish the rib-hip connection. Hold a water bottle in both hands. Lift your upper body off the floor.

2 Keep your shoulders relaxed and really lift up as you move obliquely across your body, extending the water bottle past the outside of your right knee.

3 Lift 4 times stretching across to the right side, then lift the water bottle directly up over your knees 5 times before you lift 4 times across to the left side.

3 Standing side reach

What it does: Stretches and tightens both sets of the oblique waist muscles.

How many you do: 4 sets of 16 repetitions on each side

1 Stand with good posture. Draw your abdominals in and focus on the rib-hip connection. Extend one arm up over your head and curl the other across in front of your body.

Cardio

Those with carrot shapes should focus on all-round activities. Team sports such as soccer, netball and hockey will provide a great aerobic workout as well as challenging co-ordination and speed. If you prefer to exercise alone, gym-based activities such as step aerobics and studio-based cardio classes may be more enjoyable. Aim to get a minimum of three structured cardio sessions in a week.

2 Stretch across to the side with your top arm, while drawing in and around the waist with your other arm. Keep movements small and controlled. Repeat on the other side.

Red pepper-shaped

You want to: firm and shape all your curves, ensuring they don't get too big.

Action The exercises in this section target more than one muscle group at a time. This helps you get an extra calorie burn effect as well as the toning benefits your body curves need.

Target Perform these exercises 4 times a week, along with your cardio programme.

1 Tricep dip with arm reach

What it does: Streamlines whole body, tightens backs of arms and firms buttocks.
How many you do: 12–16 repetitions.

1 Start sitting on the edge of a chair. Rest the heels of your hands on the chair with your fingers pointing down towards the floor.

2 Support your weight on your hands and lower yourself down for a tricep dip, keeping your elbows pointing backwards. Don't go too low.

3 Straighten your arms again then press your hips forward and stretch one arm diagonally over your head.

2 Four point lunge

What it does: Shapes, strengthens and lengthens the thigh. A great exercise that uses virtually all the thigh muscles.

How many you do: 12 slow repetitions on each side.

1 Stand on the floor (or on a low bench or bottom stair).

2 Extend one leg back a large stride behind you. The front knee will be slightly bent. Lower the back knee to the floor.

Top tip: Check the front knee is directly over your ankle and not pushing forwards over your toe. Also check the knee is not rolling inwards. If you draw an imaginary line down your knee cap and through to your foot, it should be in line with your second toe. If you find it difficult to balance during the four point lunge, rest your hands on the back of a chair.

3 Straighten your back knee then step forwards and stand up straight again, on the count of 4. Repeat on the other side, keeping your movements slow and controlled.

3 Modified teaser

What it does: Flattens and firms whole of abdominal area.
How many you do: 12–16 repetitions.

1 Lie on your back with your knees bent and your hands on the floor by your thighs. Establish the rib-hip connection, making sure you can feel your abdominals working.

2 Lift your upper body off the floor and place your hands on your outer thighs. Hold for a count of 4 then extend your arms over your head before returning them to the start position.

Apple-shaped

You want to: flatten abdominals that refuse to be trained! Downsize your midriff.

Action These effective abdominal exercises will reap dividends for both male and female apple shapes. Make sure you always establish the rib-hip connection (see page 76) before you start, to avoid straining your lower back.

Target Do them 6 times a week. The abdominal muscle responds particularly well to being trained nearly every day – but do remember to have that rest day. Combine this with your regular cardio programme and you should soon see a difference.

1 Ab curl with towel

What it does: Tightens upper abdominals, especially around the rib area.
How many you do: 16 repetitions

1 Lie on the floor with your knees bent. Place a rolled-up towel on the floor between your bottom and your feet, slightly in front of your extended fingers. Slide your feet away from your bottom until you feel your toes start to come off the floor. Establish the rib-hip connection.

2 Slowly curl up from the breast bone and lift your fingers over the top of the towel to touch the floor on the other side. The emphasis should be on tucking the ribs underneath you, rather than lifting them up.

2 Bridge with leg point

What it does: Lengthens the abdominals while firming them.
How many you do: Complete 6 times with each leg.

1 Lie on your back on the floor, with you spine in neutral position and knees bent. Position the legs far enough away from your bottom so you just start to feel your toes come off the floor. Pull down through your belly button, so your tummy muscles are contracted before you even start to lift.

2 Peel your back off the floor one vertebra at a time. Start slowly and use your abdominals to create the movement. Hold your abs in tight at the top of the movement and press your knees away from you, making a bridge shape.

3 Extend one leg straight outwards, keeping your knees together and your abdominals firmly contracted.

4 Lift the leg from the hip and point the toe, then lower again. Slowly lower your upper body down to the floor, using your abdominals to control the movement.

3 Ab curl with single leg drop

What it does: Firms and flattens all the abdominals; it is particularly effective on the difficult lower belly area.

How many you do: This is hard; build up to 12 repetitions, lowering both the right and the left leg each time.

Cardio

Power walking and Astanga yoga are the best cardio combination for apple shapes. Power walking will provide the greater challenge, while the physically demanding nature and rotational twists of Astanga yoga will improve your body awareness in your midriff and reduce your body fat. Stress can make you lay down fat in your midriff, so use exercise to help deal with the stress in your life.

1 Lie on your back and establish the rib-hip connection. Lift your legs so that they are bent directly above your hips, with your shins parallel to the floor.

2 Support your head in your hands and curl your upper body off the floor. You should feel your abdominals working.

3 Slowly lower your right leg down to the floor, gently touch it, then lift up again and lower the left leg. If you find this difficult, try keeping your shoulders on the floor throughout.

5 what you eat

Creating an Energy Gap through diet

You've just come in from an invigorating bike ride, you've worked up a huge appetite and reckon you deserve a treat. But before you get to the fridge, stop and think! Creating an Energy Gap with activity is only half the story. You can easily destroy all your good work by making the wrong food choices.

In this chapter I'll explain how you create an Energy Gap through diet. You'll find some great recipes as well as a variety of different menu plans that you can follow or adapt for yourself. Although establishing healthier eating habits is your ultimate goal, we also want to boost your energy levels. If you can keep these high, then following a sensible eating pattern and sticking to it becomes a lot easier. First of all, let's look at what comprises a healthy diet.

Foods contain five classes of nutrients: carbohydrates, fats, proteins, vitamins and minerals. They also contain water, which is essential for all your body's processes, and fibre, which is necessary to keep your digestive system functioning smoothly. Carbohydrates, fats and proteins provide the substratum the body needs to give it energy. These are called macronutrients. Vitamins and minerals have no calorific value, but are nevertheless essential for the breakdown of macronutrients.

Carbohydrates

What they are Carbohydrates form the backbone of our diet. Fruit, vegetables, simple sugars such as biscuits and cakes, and starchy carbs such as potatoes, rice and bread are all carbohydrate-rich foods. Carbohydrates are usually classified as either simple or complex, according to their chemical structure. Recently, carbohydrates have been classified according to the Glycaemic Index as well (see page 104).

Why you need them Carbohydrate-rich foods supply the body with its primary source of fuel – glucose. Glucose is a type of sugar that the body can easily use and transport (when we talk about blood sugars, we are actually talking about our blood glucose levels). Glucose can also be stored in the muscles as glycogen and is the main source of fuel for the nervous system and brain. Carbohydrates must be present for us to burn body fat; but any excess calories from carbohydrates will be converted to and stored as body fat in our fat cells.

How much do we need? Some health institutions and nutritionists recommend that we obtain between 50 and 65 per cent of our calorie intake from carbs, but more recent guidelines are based on body weight per kilogram: 4–5g of carbohydrate per kg of body weight for healthy, active people. The recent popularity of high-protein, low-carb diets has misled many of us into cutting out carbs altogether. A moderate reduction is probably beneficial to weight loss, but banning carbs totally is ultimately detrimental to health and energy levels. Implementing a 'Carb Curfew', however – avoiding starchy carbs after 5pm – can be an effective, simple and easy way to achieve a better balance of nutrients (see page 116).

Carbohydrates are made up of sugars, and many of us are still confused as to how much and what kind of sugar to consume. There is no simple answer. Surprisingly, there is no scientific relationship between sugar intake and excess weight, but what we do know is that consuming too many calories contributes to obesity and that many foods high in sugar are also high in fat. There is some preliminary evidence to support a link between high sugar intake and increased levels of fats in the blood in overweight people.

While there is no universally accepted recommended daily allowance for the amount of sugar in the diet, it is advisable to make reductions where you can, specifically avoiding refined foods such as biscuits, cakes and sweets. Processed and pre-prepared products often do not distinguish between added and naturally occurring sugars on their labels, so try to avoid them where possible. These added sugars can pose a risk to dental health, and therefore should be particularly restricted in children's diets.

What is the Glycaemic Index?

The Glycaemic Index (GI) ranks carbohydrate-containing foods according to blood glucose response after ingestion. This rating is a useful tool for weight management since it can help maintain and stabilise energy levels, curbing hunger pangs and sugar urges. Several factors can influence GI so it is not easily predicted and cannot be determined by whether a carbohydrate is simple (such as fruit or table sugar) or complex (such as bread or potatoes). For example, an apple (simple carbohydrate) has a low GI while the GI of bread is high. Low GI foods have a value of less than 55, moderate GI foods between 56 and 69, and high GI foods have GI more than 70. The ratings are based on ingestion of 50g.

Some GI comparisons

Breads

Baguette	95
Gluten-free bread	90
Black rye bread	76
Bagels	72
White rolls	61
Granary bread	61
Stoneground bread	59
Sourdough bread	57
Pitta bread	57
Oatcakes	54
Rye bread	51
Pumpernickel	50
Fruit tea bread	47

Desserts

Rice pudding	81
Sponge cake with cream	67
Vanilla ice cream	61
Banana	55
Plain yoghurt	46
Orange	44
Custard	43
Apple	38
Fruit yoghurt	33
Cherries	22

Carb Foods

White rice	87
Baked potatoes	85
Chips	75
Taco shells	68
Polenta	68
Couscous	65
Basmati rice	58
Egg noodles	46
Durum-wheat spaghetti	41
Mung bean noodles	39
Pearl barley	25

Drinks

Glucose drink	95
Beer	88
Fizzy orange drink	68
Lemon squash	66
Cola	53
Orange juice	50
Apple juice	40
Tomato juice	38
Skimmed milk	32
Tea	0
Water	0

You can make the Glycaemic Index work for you by choosing low to moderate GI carbs, and you can make some of your favourite high GI carbs behave like a low GI carb, stabilising your energy levels, by adding a serving of protein.

Fats

What they are The fat in our food is the most concentrated source of energy, providing 9 calories per gram, more than twice as many as either protein or carbohydrate. Foods such as butter, oils, nuts, cheese and coconuts are all rich sources of fat. There are three main sub-groups, divided according to their chemical structure: saturated, polyunsaturated and monounsaturated.

Why we need them It is important to stress that some fat is crucial for good health. Certain foods supply the fat-soluble vitamins A, D, E and K, as well as some essential fats, which the body cannot make for itself. Fat helps us to transport important antioxidants and to produce key hormones that regulate various body processes. If we cut out all fat in our diet, we would be depriving ourselves of vital nutrients.

Saturated fats

These are the least healthy, and have no useful function. Eating too much saturated fat is associated with an increased risk of heart disease. When we eat food that is high in saturated fat, the simplest thing for our body to do with it is transport it to the fat cells, and dump it there. Quite simply, the fat cells welcome the saturated fat we eat with open arms – they get bigger and bigger, our clothes get tighter and tighter and our health risks get higher and higher. Saturated fats include butter, lard, cheese and fat on meat.

Polyunsaturated fats

These essential fats help us to burn energy from other foods such as proteins and carbohydrates. They play an important role in the healthy functioning of our body before what remains of them is transported to the fat cells and stored. They are subdivided into two groups:

Omega 3 essential fats These are found in oily fish such as salmon, herring, sardines, trout, pilchards and mackerel, flaxseed and pumpkin seed. They are thought to help to prevent atherosclerosis, lower blood pressure and reduce

Good fat

Bad fat

blood fat (making the blood less sticky and thereby less susceptible to clotting). Eating three servings of oily fish a week, or using flaxseed oil in your salad dressing will help you hit your Omega 3 fatty acid quota.

Omega 6 essential fats These are found mainly in hemp, pumpkin, sunflower, safflower, sesame and corn oil. About half of the oils found in these seeds come from Omega 6 fatty acids. They help prevent blood clots, lower blood pressure, maintain water balance in the body and stabilise blood sugar levels. However, excessive consumption may reduce beneficial high-density lipoproteins or HDLs, and exacerbate the damage done by potentially cancer-causing free radicals.

Monounsaturated fats

These are regarded as the most healthy fats, partly because research has shown that Mediterranean diets, rich in olive oil, are associated with the lowest risks of heart disease. However, bear in mind that a tablespoon of olive oil has the same number of calories as a tablespoon of melted lard! So the total amount of fat still has to be taken into account. Monounsaturated fats are liquid at room temperature and because they are more stable than polyunsaturated fats, are a better choice for cooking oil. Rapeseed oil also contains monounsaturated fat.

Trans/hydrogenated fats

You may well have come across the term 'trans fats' or 'hydrogenated fats'. These fats are particularly unhealthy.

Storage and cooking

- Keep flaxseed oil in a cupboard, as it can be damaged by exposure to light.
- Omega 3 fats can be damaged by excessive heat, so avoid cooking with these fats at high temperatures

They often started out as polyunsaturated fat, but after processing at very high temperatures, their chemical structure made them less stable and they became damaged. Consumption is associated with an increased risk of cancers and heart disease. They are found in margarine and processed foods. Look for the word 'hydrogenated' on your food labels and you have found trans fats!

Type of fat	Where you find it	Health Rating
Monounsaturated fats	Olive oil	Excellent
	Canola	
	Olives	
	Nuts	
	Avocados	
Polyunsaturated	Corn oil	Good
	Sunflower oil	
	Sesame oil	
	Seeds	
Saturated fats	Butter/dairy products	Unhealthy: restrict to
	Lard	less than 10g a day
	Meat	
	Eggs	
Hydrogenated fats	Vegetable shortening	Bad: avoid these
	Palm oil	
	Margarine	

According to new dietary recommendations, fat should constitute no more than 30 per cent of total calorie intake, and 10 per cent or less should come from saturated sources. If you are adhering to a 1,600-calorie a day diet, for example, this equates to 50–60g of fat per day in total, of which a maximum of 20g should be saturated.

Proteins

What they are

Proteins are made up of chains of amino acids. There are hundreds of amino acids in nature, but only 23 are important to humans, and of these, 8 are termed 'essential', as we cannot manufacture them in the body, and therefore need to absorb them from the foods we eat. Meat, fish, pulses and dairy products are all foods with a high protein content.

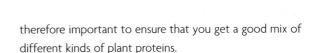

Why you need them

Proteins are essential for tissue repair, maintenance and growth, making up part of every cell in the body. A regular supply of protein is required for growth processes, and to repair bodily wear and tear. Protein can be divided into two groups: dairy products, which include milk, cheese and yoghurt, and non-dairy sources, which include meat, fish, nuts, seeds and eggs, pulses and beans. The important role that protein plays means that it is much harder for the body to store excess protein as fat.

How much do we need?

The Foods Standards Agency recommends that we obtain 15 per cent of our energy from protein. This amount is adequate for health purposes, but a higher intake is preferable if you want to restrict your calorie intake. Another way of determining your protein needs is by body weight: guidelines suggest aiming for 0.75g of protein per kg of body weight, so if you weigh 70kg you eat 52.5g of protein a day. It is important, however, that this is obtained from fish, lean meat sources, nuts and seeds, and balanced with plenty or fruits and vegetables.

Protein in the vegetarian diet

If you are a vegetarian or vegan, you will need to take a little more care with your protein intake, as plant protein sources (such as legumes, nuts and seeds) may not contain all the amino acids you need. It is therefore important to ensure that you get a good mix of different kinds of plant proteins.

Protein for athletes

If you are an athlete or involved in regular intense exercise, you will have a greater protein requirement, as extra protein is needed for muscle repair and recovery after training. However, studies have shown that you only need between 1.2–1.4g per kg of body weight to meet the demands of an average strength or endurance training programme: any amount above this provides no additional benefit.

Dietary fibre

What it is Dietary fibre is the indigestible part of our food that helps our digestive system to function smoothly. There are two types of dietary fibre: soluble and insoluble.

Soluble fibre Dissolved in water, this forms a gel. Found in fruits, vegetables, legumes and oat bran, it helps reduce cholesterol when consumed as part of a diet low in saturated fat. Soluble fibre can also help control blood sugar levels.

Insoluble fibre This fibre cannot dissolve in water, but instead absorbs water as it passes through the body and contributes to faecal bulk. It's found in fruits, vegetables, whole grains and wheat bran.

Why we need it A high-fibre diet is important for several reasons: it can give your energy levels a boost, and helps lower

the risk of diabetes, heart disease and possibly cancer. And – probably most important to you right now – it can help you to control your weight. Fibre slows digestion and makes you feel full, so it's a useful tool to use – but it will take a minimum of six servings of fruits and veggies and three servings of whole grains daily to meet recommendations.

Studies show that certain types of fibre lower cholesterol, normalise blood sugar in diabetics and, of course, help with digestive regularity. Regular movements are not only important for bowel health but also improve mood.

Juicing

Juicing fruits and vegetables is a great way to get an antioxidant blast as well as helping you to fulfil your fruit and vegetable quota. While your palate will eventually grow to savour all-veggie juices, they can be tough for beginners. These easy-to-love recipes add fruit for natural sweetness.

The Basic Cocktail: *juice 3 carrots, 2 stalks celery, a 2.5cm piece of ginger and half an apple. It's a good souce of betacarotene and zinc, and boosts the immune system.*

The Pick-me-up: *juice 3 carrots, 2 fennel stalks with leaves and half a lemon. Relieves fatigue and releases feel-good brain chemicals.*

Vitamins and minerals

Vitamins and minerals are vital components in our daily diet. While they provide no direct energy in the form of calories, they do play a very important role, as they are essential in the breakdown of macronutrients for the release of energy. Since they only need to be consumed in small quantities, they are often referred to as 'micronutrients'. To help ensure that you are getting an adequate supply of vitamins and minerals, have a look at the quick-reference table on pages 110–11, which will inform you of the benefits of your favourite fruits, vegetables and other foods. Remember: food doesn't just meet your energy needs, but can directly affect your health and looks as well. Some diets advise you to take vitamin/mineral supplements while you are following them, but I always find this suspicious. A good balanced diet with fresh, unprocessed foods should provide the micronutrients you need, unless you are recovering from illness, pregnant or elderly.

Healthy eating and weight management

Getting your head around nutrients need not be confusing: the most important thing is to ensure calorie intake is managed while you're still consuming proper levels of essential nutrients. Select a variety of foods, especially those that are nutrient-dense yet low in calories.

And remember: • *Eat lots of fruits and vegetables* • *Fill up on fibre* • *Avoid saturated fats* • *Drink lots of water* • *Choose lean proteins*

Vitamins and their function in the body

Vitamin	Found in	Functions in the body
Vitamin A (retinol)	Dairy products, green leafy vegetables, yellow and orange fruits, fortified cereals and oatmeals	Promotes healthy growth, maintains vision, skin cells, gut and respiratory tract.
Vitamin B1 (thiamin)	All vegetables, fortified cereals and oatmeal, whole grains, rice and pasta, meat	Maintenance of healthy nervous system, heart and growth. Involved in carbohydrate metabolism and energy production.
Vitamin B2 (riboflavin):	Green leafy vegetables, whole grains, organ meats	Helps the body release energy from protein, fats and carbohydrates during metabolism.
Vitamin B3 (niacin)	Fortified cereals and oatmeal, meat and poultry	Involved in carbohydrate, protein and fat metabolism.
Vitamin B6 (pyridoxine)	Whole grains, meats, poultry, fish	Aids both glucose and protein metabolism and energy production, maintains healthy nervous system. Important in resistance to infection.
Vitamin B12 (cobalamin)	Meat, seafood	Aids cell development, functioning of the nervous system and the metabolism of protein and fat.
Vitamin C (ascorbic acid)	Citrus fruits, berries	Essential for structure of bones, cartilage, muscle and blood vessels, helps maintain capillaries and gums and aids iron absorption.
Vitamin D (calciferol)	Dairy products, fish	Aids bone and tooth formation, helps maintain healthy functioning of the heart and nervous system.
Vitamin E (alpha-tocopherol)	Green leafy vegetables, fortified cereals and oatmeal, grain products, vegetable oils, nuts	Protects blood cells, body tissue and essential fatty acids from damage or destruction in the body.
Vitamin K	Green leafy vegetables, fruits, grain products, vegetable oils, nuts	Essential for blood clotting.
Biotin	Fortified cereals and oatmeals, grain products, vegetable oils, nuts, whole grains, organ meats	Involved in metabolism of protein, fats and carbohydrates.

Vitamin	Found in	Functions in the body
Calcium	Milk and milk products	Essential for healthy bones and teeth. Important in muscle contraction and the transmission of nerve impulses.
Chromium	Whole grains, corn oil, clams, brewer's yeast	Important in glucose metabolism (energy), increases effectiveness of insulin.
Folate (folacin, folic acid)	Green leafy vegetables, organ meats	Aids genetic material development, involved in red blood cell production, and strengthens immune system
Iodine	Legumes, nuts, oysters, organ meats, seafood	Formation of red blood cells, bone growth and health. Works with Vitamin C to form elastin. Component of hormone thyroxine which controls metabolism.
Iron	Legumes, meats	Essential in red blood cell formation. Improves blood quality, increases resistance to stress and disease.
Magnesium	Green vegetables	Acid/alkaline balance, important in metabolism of carbohydrates, minerals and sugar.
Manganese	Whole grains, nuts	Enzyme activation, carbohydrates and fat production, sex hormone production, skeletal development.
Pantothenic acid	All vegetables, fruits, whole grains, meats	Aids the release of energy from fats and carbohydrates.
Phosphorus	Milk and milk products, eggs, grains, meat, poultry, fish	Important role in the delivery of energy to all cells, and formation of bones and teeth.
Potassium	All vegetables (particularly potatoes and tomatoes), lean meats	Maintenance of body fluids, controls activity of heart muscle, nervous system and kidneys.
Selenium	Grains, seafood, organ meats, lean meats	Protects body tissues against oxidative damage from radiation, pollution and normal metabolic processing.
Zinc	Eggs, whole grains, seafood, organ meats, lean meats	Involved in digestion and metabolism, important in development of reproductive system, aids healing.

Water

No natural resource is undervalued as much as fresh water. Nothing will have a greater immediate impact on your energy levels. If you drink less than eight glasses (2 litres) of water a day, your body may be chronically dehydrated. You will lack energy and your brain will misinterpret this tiredness and crave a sugary energy boost. Don't think you can quench your thirst with tea, coffee or colas – these will leave you dehydrated as well. Pure, clean water is the best drink of all.

Why is water important? Water is crucial to every single process that occurs in our bodies. Every cell is bathed in water and every chemical or physiological reaction in our body requires its presence. If your body is even slightly dehydrated, you are asking it to perform in an environment that is not totally supportive to what it needs to do.

Why is water particularly important for weight management? Water swells food cells and helps our body take up vital nutrients. It also makes us feel more satisfied. It bulks up food, stretching the stomach wall and sending messages to the brain telling us we are full. In addition, the water content in blood helps the absorption and transportation of all the nutrients, vitamins and minerals we have consumed (fat can only be broken down in the presence of water), and flushes waste products away. This is essential for your weight loss journey, because when you make the change to healthier eating, your body will initially produce more toxins, which will need to be flushed out.

Water also retrains your thoughts from hunger to thirst. The hypothalmus, the regulatory part of the brain, sends out messages telling us whether we are hungry or thirsty; sadly, however, if we become dehydrated, we lose the ability to understand the true message our hypothalamus is sending us.

Sodium and salt

From a health perspective, the amount of salt in our food is something we should all be aware of.

What it is Sodium is a calorie-free mineral that works its way into the diet in the form of salt. But we are not just talking saltshaker here – it is estimated that about 75 per cent of the sodium in our diet comes from processed foods.

Why we need it We do need a certain amount of salt for our bodies to function smoothly – to keep nerve pathways working and to maintain our muscles. But too much salt has been clearly linked with hypertension (it raises blood pressure), which in turn increases the risk of heart disease or stroke (Britain's biggest killers). It is currently thought that we are each consuming in the region of 9g of salt a day, which is about 2 teaspoons. The Food Standards Agency is so alarmed by this figure that it is lobbying the food industry to reduce the amount of salt in processed food.

How much do we need? Everyone should lower their sodium intake to 1,500mg daily (half a teaspoon of salt contains about 1,200mg of sodium). Try cooking with spices, herbs, lemon and salt-free seasoning blends to reduce sodium intake – and remember to read those labels!

Choose sea salt

While table salt (sodium chloride) is responsible for raising blood pressure and causing heart problems, natural sea salt is health-promoting, since it contains many other minerals, including magnesium and calcium. It is the healthy alternative to sodium chloride, so use it when cooking and on food instead of table salt. Up to 5g (a teaspoon) per day is considered safe.

How much should I drink? Research suggests we need 1ml of fluid per calorie we consume. So if your average daily intake is 1,600 calories, you need a minimum of 1.6 litres of water. While a healthy diet containing lots of fruit and vegetables can provide a proportion of this fluid, we should supplement these sources with drinking water itself.

And when? Spread your water intake evenly throughout the day. If you're observing the 2-litre recommendation, that's a half-litre by lunchtime, a further litre by late afternoon and the remainder in the evening. You may find that initially this new regime will have you running to the loo, but as your body adjusts, the effect will wear off.

The tell-tale signs of a fad diet

Fad diets tend to capture media attention, but as we've seen, they're the One-Night Stands of weight loss. Your brain cannot enjoy a lasting relationship with your body when you're following a fad diet. At best, you'll regain the weight you've lost; at worst, you could damage your health. To become a fad-diet detective, look out for warning signs. **They often:** promote magic or miracle foods, promise rapid weight loss, provide no exercise advice, stipulate bizarre quantities or specific food combinations, exclude entire food groups or prescribe rigid menus.

You may recognise some of the following.

Food combining

Claims: eating protein and carbohydrates in the same meal disrupts the digestion and produces toxins that make you fat; carbohydrates raise insulin levels, increase appetite and encourage fat storage, resulting in weight gain.

Reality check The science aside, just ensuring you do not combine protein and carbohydrate in one meal is hard enough. For every meal, every day, it's next to impossible. Such a diet cannot be sustained in the long term. To make diets work, they have to fit in with your life.

High-protein, low carb

Claims: an excessive amount of insulin is released after you eat carbohydrate foods and this increases fat storage in the body; sugar and refined carbs are bad for your health, energy levels, mental state and sex life! Often, in the first two weeks of a low-carb plan, you're allowed only 20g of carbohydrate a day, so if you eat a banana, which has 30g of carbs, you've blown it already. You progress to 40g of carbs a day and then to the maintenance level of 60g. Consequently, these diets tend to offer very limited food choices, while encouraging high protein and fat consumption. These diets also claim they dissolve fat tissue and thereby trigger more fat loss.

Reality check No food is bad for your health when eaten in moderation. The World Health Organisation confirms the importance of carbs in the diet and research has shown that diets high in saturated fat can increase risks of obesity, cardio-vascular disease and certain cancers. Ketosis, the bodily process resulting from excess protein intake and depletion of carbohydrates, can suppress appetite, but the side-effects are nausea, dizziness and bad breath.

Sugarbusters/sugar cravers

Claims: eating high Glycaemic Index carbs increases insulin and promotes body fat storage and obesity; fluids drunk with meals inhibit digestion and encourage fat storage. Some of these diets try to eliminate all carbs, so that calories are only obtained from protein and fat, and you are only allowed a very low calorie intake (between 800 and 1,200 a day).

Reality check Weight loss results from calorie reduction, not a decrease in insulin levels. There is no scientific evidence that fluids drunk with meals inhibit digestion.

The Zone

Claims: each meal should be composed of an optimum nutrient mix of 30 per cent fat, 30 per cent protein and 40 per cent carbs. This is the body's 'Zone', where body and mind are united for optimum performance and optimum weight loss.

Reality check While this diet does at least advocate drinking water and taking exercise, it is complicated in practice. This 'macronutrient block method', as it is called, has a very rigid structure, with little flexibility, and views food purely as a drug.

Never say 'no' Nearly all foods can be fair game. Even when you're trying to restrict calories, indulging in a favourite treat is okay as long as portion sizes are controlled and it does not become a regular luxury. Likewise, don't develop a phobia for a food, food group or component of food. Avoiding carbohydrates, fruits, sugars, protein or fat – whatever the fad diet of the moment may be – is a bad idea; instead, moderation is the key.

So... how many calories do you need?

If you are	Your activity factor is
Sedentary woman	12
Sedentary man	14
Active woman	15
Active man	17
Very active woman	18
Very active man	20

You discovered how physically active you are back in Chapter 3 (see page 48). A simple way to calculate how many calories you need is to use the above table to find your activity factor. Multiply your activity factor by your current weight in pounds. The resulting number is the approximate number of calories you currently need to maintain your weight. The maths looks like this:

Activity factor x weight in pounds = current energy needs.
For example, an active woman who weighs 150lb would need 2,250 calories a day (15 x 150 = 2,250).

If you want to achieve safe, effective weight loss, reduce your result by 500, and that will give you your new target. A reduction of 1,000 calories a day is achievable, but it will be a significant decrease that will probably feel quite hard to maintain, so start with 500 calories – you can always cut back further once your new eating habits have evolved.
Note: Never take in fewer than 1,500 calories per day unless under medical supervision.

How can I help myself cut calories?

The following principles will help you reach your weight loss destination. Remember that people who've got there and stayed there do not continually count calories, but they are calorie aware – and you will start to develop these skills too as you put the principles in practice.

Introduce the Carb Curfew

Carb Curfew means no starchy carbs – bread, pasta, rice, potatoes or cereal – after 5pm. Don't panic – you won't feel as if you're about to starve, since there are still plenty of filling foods to eat. You can incorporate a whole variety of nutritious foods in your evening meal, including lean meat and fish, fruit, vegetables, pulses and dairy products, and come up with something absolutely delicious! Turn to the dinner recipe ideas on pages 142–63 and you'll see what I mean.

Many of my clients consider the Carb Curfew to be the single most important tool in their weight management success and I know it can help you too. The Carb Curfew helps you control your insulin levels, which means it's easier to stabilise your energy levels – important for weight loss.

Why?

● It's an easy way to create an Energy Gap! You will be cutting down on calories and filling up slow-releasing, energy-providing pulses, so you'll feel less hungry and more energetic.
● Substituting fruit and vegetables instead of rice or pasta will increase your vitamin and mineral intake, which is important for the breakdown of macronutrients.
● It reduces bloating. As your body digests and stores carbohydrate, it breaks it down into glucose and either stores it as glycogen in the muscles or as fat in the fat cells. Storing those starchy carbs as glycogen is your body's preferred choice but to do this it has to store three units of water with every one unit of glycogen. The net result is a bloated tummy.
● It prevents food hangovers. If you stuff your face at night, you will wake up with a 'food hangover' and won't want breakfast. By the evening, you'll be starving again.

Include protein in every meal

Although many nutritionists are still wary about the potential dangers of high-protein diets, consuming slightly more protein than you normally would can be an effective tool for weight loss, as it helps you feel fuller for longer.

Why?

● Protein contains an essential amino acid called leucine, a muscle regulator vital to weight loss that can be obtained only from protein sources.
● Protein helps blunt the rise in blood sugar after a meal or snack, so it gives you staying power.
● Protein stimulates the release of dopamine, which is a brain transmitter that actually makes you feel more alert. It boosts concentration and curbs lethargy.

Lower your fat intake

There is continued debate over whether a low-fat diet (less than 25 per cent of total calories) contributes to successful weight management because good sources of fat actually help your body burn off other calories. The important thing is to cut down on the bad fats but keep enough of the good ones.

Why?

● Research has found that simply lowering dietary fat intake promotes weight loss because you take in far fewer calories.
● High fat foods are not very filling, so you're more likely to over-eat, yet a small amount of fat provides a high number of calories. It's a lose–lose situation!

Stop Portion Distortion

One of the main reasons we are gaining weight is that we are over-eating. Portion sizes in restaurants and fast-food outlets have increased eightfold in the past 20 years, as companies vie with each other to lure consumers with ever-bigger promises of value for money. When serving sizes are bigger and bigger, it becomes difficult to decide what a 'normal' portion is.

Why?

● It allows you to eat the things you like, as long as you control the amount you're eating.
● Excess food means excess calories

BODY LAID BARE...

Stopping Portion Distortion – a few tips

Weighing out the correct portion of food – 80g of meat, for example – can be a bore, so let's make things simple. To keep your meals in check, compile a handy Portion Distortion basket in your kitchen. Put in it some everyday items that are the same size as the portion of food you should be eating. Soon you'll become familiar with the sizes, so you'll be able to stop Portion Distortion wherever you are – in a restaurant you can order what you want but only eat as much as the size of the healthy portion. If self-control is going to be a problem, then order just a starter instead, or share your food with a friend. Watching the size of your portions is an invaluable piece of weight-loss advice. You can still eat the foods you like, so you don't feel deprived, but you have control over what you consume and the number of calories you take in. Use the following objects to judge the portion size you should be aiming at.

Think...	For...
Two dice	Nuts and cheese
Deck of cards	Meat and fish
Teaspoon	Oils and fats
Tennis ball	Vegetables
Golf ball	Uncooked rice or coucous
Computer mouse	Cooked portion of starchy carbs

Front-load your day

Starve yourself all day in the belief that you are creating a huge Energy Gap, and you're heading for disaster: under-eating by day only leads to over-eating in the evening. Eat a good, slow-energy-releasing breakfast every day, however, and you'll be on the right track immediately. Don't worry – it doesn't have to be first thing in the morning.

Why?

● It helps stabilise your energy levels. When you are hungry you will find yourself unable to make sensible food choices, and when you start eating again you'll find it harder to tell when you've had enough.

● Eating your food when your body needs it will encourage you to spread your calories evenly throughout the day. This way, you'll burn more calories through the Thermic Effect of Food, and you'll have lasting energy.

Limit alcohol

Alcohol is a hidden pound-piler, although the good news is that losing weight doesn't mean giving up alcohol for life, just moderating your intake. From a health perspective, 'moderate' is equivalent to two drinks per day. From a weight perspective, if you can cut down on that, you will be making a significant saving in calories – and at particular stages of your weight loss journey cutting it out completely can be a big bonus.

Why?

● Alcohol is high in calories. A 500ml bottle of lager contains approximately 145 calories and a double measure of whisky (50ml) is 112 calories. Alcohol cannot be used directly by the muscles – it travels straight into the bloodstream, where it has to be metabolised before the body can convert it into fuel sources such as carbohydrate or fat. Research also suggests that a glass of wine may contribute more to your waistline than a slice of cake with the same number of calories.

● It weakens your calorie awareness, so self-discipline goes out the window and you tend to pick poor-quality foods.

● A study in the *American Journal of Clinical Nutrition* found that just a single glass of pre-lunch wine or beer left volunteers feeling less satisfied after their meal, and increased calorie intake over the next 24 hours.

Have more liquid-based foods

Try to incorporate more soups, juices and smoothies as well as water-based vegetables and fruit into your diet. Liquid-based food doesn't mean liquid lunches, however!

Why?

● Foods with a high water content help stave off hunger and make you feel full. Studies have shown that dieters who follow this advice tend to stick to their diet plan without feeling unsatisfied or deprived.

BODY LAID BARE...

Alcohol and your health The good news is that there are some health benefits to be had from drinking alcohol in moderate amounts. A recent study from the University of Alabama reported that moderate consumption of alcohol may decrease production and circulating levels by up to 20 per cent of a clotting protein called fibrinogen – high levels of which are associated with coronary artery, cerebrovascular and peripheral vascular diseases. Other research associates moderate alcohol intake with a lower risk of gallstones. Chronic heavy drinking, on the other hand, is a leading cause of several cardiovascular illnesses, including high blood pressure, as well as diseases of the liver and gastrointestinal organs. Research has also shown that it may be harmful to bones. A significant reduction in bone remodelling – the process of replacing old bone with new – occurs when alcohol is consumed in moderate or high amounts.

Tips for healthy drinking

● Watch the size of your glass! Most pubs and bars serve wine in 175ml or even 250ml glasses, but an official 'unit' of wine is actually just 125ml of 9 per cent alcohol wine. It's easy to go overboard without realising it if you drink from a larger glass, or if you drink stronger wine – a 125ml glass of wine with 12 per cent alcohol is actually 1.5 units. Half a pint of ordinary strength lager or bitter (3.5 per cent alcohol) and a single measure of spirits (40 per cent alcohol) are one unit each.

● The Department of Health guidelines stipulate that women should drink a maximum of 3 units per day and men 4 units, although their weekly guidelines are 14 units for women and 21 for men – so they assume that people will not drink their full quota every day.

● If you drink three units of red wine a day you are clocking up an extra 255 calories. If you drink four units of lager, you're consuming 400 calories. Three gin and diet tonics could mean an additional 255 calories a day – or 1,785 in a week. You'd have to do a lot of extra aerobic activity to burn all those off!

● While it's good to have a few alcohol-free days each week, don't 'save up' your units for a binge on Friday night – this overstresses the liver and is likely to lead to low energy levels and poor eating habits (like that curry or burger take-away on the way home from the pub).

● Mix alcoholic drinks with soft drinks or water to pace yourself and prevent dehydration.

● Don't eat crisps or nuts while you're drinking alcohol – the salt will make you thirstier so you'll drink more.

● Do not drink on an empty stomach. This will slow down the rate at which your body can metabolise alcohol and you will feel drunk very quickly.

● Be extra careful if you are short, very overweight, particularly run down or tired, as your body will be less alcohol-tolerant. Women may also find their tolerance is lower while they are menstruating.

The Menu Plans

The Menu Plans have been devised so that you can choose from a selection of breakfasts, lunches, dinners

and snacks grouped according to their calorie content (you'll find all the recipes at the end of the chapter).

Make your choices from the lists so that in total they add up to your personal daily calorie limit.

Try to spread your calories evenly throughout the day. For example, if your new daily calorie intake is 1,800, you may choose to organise your calories in the following way:

- **Breakfast** = 500 calories
- **Lunch** = 500 calories
- **Snack** = 300 calories
- **Dinner** = 500 calories

Remember to eat!

If you are not consuming enough calories, your metabolism will be alerted to the possibility of an imminent food shortage and possible starvation! It will automatically slow down as the self-preservation instinct kicks in (that is, it gets better at holding on to the fat you have stored up). It's probable as well that you won't be getting enough of the nutrients you need – your health will suffer and your energy levels flag.

Meal goals

When you're planning a day's meals, bear the following meal goals in mind, and choose foods that will keep your energy levels high all day long.

Breakfast To help you become alert after your mini-hibernation. Make sure you eat some protein and a small portion of carbohydrates to round out your meal.

Breakfast

200 or less	300 or less	Around 400
Banana-chocolate smoothie (see page 225)	Banana-sour cherry bread (see page 225)	Low-fat natural yoghurt with granola and apple purée (see page 128)
Moosewood sesame citrus delight (see page 124)	Poached egg on Marmite toast with fresh orange juice (see page 128)	Date and pumpkin seed brunch loaf (see page 127)
Poached egg, tomato, mushrooms and whole-meal toast (see page 129)	Fruity English muffin (see page 129)	Pinhead oatmeal porridge with raisins (see page 124)
Medium slice melon and 100g plain cottage cheese	Cereal with milk and fruit (see page 129)	Blueberry-yoghurt slush with granola (see page 128)
100g natural low-fat bio yoghurt and 70g strawberries	Raspberry smoothie (see page 129)	Banana muffins (see page 127)
1 slice wholemeal toast and a medium banana	Breakfast on the go (see page 129)	Peanut butter toast and a piece of fruit (see page 129)

Lunch Head off a slump and stay sharp. Focus on your meal, eat a lot of vegetables, a deck-of-cards size portion of protein and a small portion of carbs (too much will make you feel tired later). Watch your fat intake – it makes you sluggish.

Afternoon snack To keep your spirits lifted until dinner. If you are having a stressful day and need a serotonin boost to calm your nerves, go the carb route. Within 30 minutes of eating carbs you will feel calmer. Think effective hydration to keep your brain in gear. If you are dragging, then have a cup of coffee or another caffeine-laced beverage. Using caffeine strategically like this can be a great help, although you should try to reduce your overall intake.

Dinner To put tension behind you, but not go to bed stuffed. Remember the Carb Curfew. If you get home hungry, have some vegetable soup: it will stave off the pangs until dinner, give you a head-start serving of vegetables and hydrate you.

Lunches

300 or less	400 or less	500 or less
Stuffed baked potatoes with sun-dried tomatoes (see page 226)	Caesar salad with Cajun grilled chicken (see page 138)	Italian-style mackerel with a tomato, anchovy and pea sauce (see page 135)
Marinated tuna steak with mushroom, parsley and lemon juice salad (see page 138)	Spicy fruity coleslaw with ham in pitta bread (see page 132)	Easy tuna melt (see page 140) with a tossed green salad on the side
Grilled teriyaki tofu with roasted red peppers and houmus roll-up (see page 131)	Trout baked in newspaper, with flaked almonds and watercress salad (see page 134)	Avocado and chicken wrap (see page 141) and a glass of fresh fruit juice
Smoked duck breast salad with griottines (see page 140)	Tuna, mushroom parsley and lemon stuffed pitta (see page 131)	Lunch on the run (see page 141) with an iced tea
Lentil salad with lardons (see page 132)	Grilled herring on oatmeal (see page 134)	A dish from the 300 or less lunches plus one from the 200 or less desserts
Open sandwich (see page 140)	Pitta Niçoise salad (see page 140)	

Dinners

300 or less	400 or less	500 or less
Easy fish and prawn curry (see page 161)	Gammon steak with Puy lentils and stir-fried greens (see page 162)	Healthy chicken nuggets with easy baked chips (see page 229)
Aromatic summer salmon with purple grape and chilli mango salsa (see page 159)	Chicken fillet en papillote with baked tomatoes and green beans (see page 145)	Thai green curry with chicken (or beef) and vegetables (see page 143)
Mexican vegetable soup (see page 153) or Gazpacho (see page 154)	Grilled salmon steak with wilted baby spinach and mushrooms (see page 160)	Chickpea and almond crêpes with courgettes and chicory (see page 158)
Baked haddock fillet with spinach (see page 160)	Tray-baked citrus chicken with lentils and rocket (see page 150)	Chilli chicken and white bean burgers with soya mayo (see page 146)
Beetroot, butternut squash, fennel and carrot with soya marinated tofu (see page 151)	Chickpea, chilli and tomato soup (see page 155)	A dish from the 300 or less dinners plus one from the 200 or less desserts
Asian-flavoured sweetcorn chowder (see page 154) or Thai vegetable soup (page 155)	Teriyaki chicken on red onion and mushrooms (see page 144)	

Snacks and desserts

100 or less	200 or less	300 or less
Apple and a matchbox-sized piece of Edam or feta cheese	200ml glass skimmed milk with 2 small cubes dark chocolate	Slice of date and pumpkin-seed brunch loaf (see page 127)
300ml glass skimmed milk	Banana-chocolate smoothie (see page 225)	Banana muffin (see page 127) with matchbox piece of cheese
Rhubarb and strawberry jelly (see page 165)	2 crispbreads with Marmite	Handful of dried fruits and nuts
Baked bananas en papillote (see page 166)	Orange, mango and passion fruit salad (see page 165)	2 crispbreads spread with half an avocado and topped with cottage cheese
Peaches baked with mascarpone (see page 167)	Cinnamon-poached fruit (see page 166)	Mango and banana smoothie (see page 129)
2 fresh figs, or a peach or a cup of cherries	Muesli bar	A small piece of chocolate chip banana snack cake (see page 167)

Your healthy eating shopping list – the basics

It's a good idea to make several copies of this list. Mark items as you run out of them and add non-essentials under 'Miscellaneous'.

Fruit and vegetables

Apples

Aubergine

Bananas

Broccoli

Cabbage (green or red)

Carrots

Cauliflower

Celery

Courgettes

Cucumbers

Fresh greens

Garlic

Grapefruit

Grapes

Lemons

Melons

Mushrooms

Onions

Oranges

Parsley

Peppers

Plums

Squash

Sweet potatoes

Meat and fish

Bacon (pork or turkey) and ham (lean)

Beef (lean minced, various lean steaks)

Chicken (skinless breasts and bone-in parts)

Lamb (chops and minced)

Pork (chops)

Salmon fillets

Haddock or other white fish fillets

Prawns

Turkey (breast, minced)

Baking aisle

Brown sugar or brown sugar substitute

Cocoa powder (unsweetened)

Olive oil

Sesame oil

Coconut (unsweetened)

Dried fruits (apricots, raisins)

Nuts (almonds, macadmia, pecans, pine nuts, pistachios, walnuts)

Peanuts, unsalted, dry-roasted

Sea salt and black pepper

Dried herbs and spices

Seeds (sesame, sunflower, pumpkin)

Canned and jarred foods

Reduced-salt stock

Dried or canned beans (black, brown lentils, chickpeas, pinto, red kidney, white)

Fish (anchovies, salmon, sardines, trout fillets, tuna in spring water or light olive oil, pilchards, skips, crab)

Fruit in fruit juice (no sugar added)

Mild green chilli peppers

Tinned tomato products

Olives

Roasted red peppers

Condiments and sauces

All-fruit spread

Hot-pepper sauce

Marinara sauce (low-sugar)

Mayonnaise (no added sugar, reduced fat)

Various mustards

Dried chilli flakes

Nut butter, natural

Pesto

Soy sauce (reduced salt)

Vinegar (cider, balsamic, red/white wine)

Thai sweet chilli sauce

Mirin (Japanese rice wine vinegar)

Rice, pasta, grains

Brown rice

Porridge oats

Pinhead oats

Pearl barley

Quinoa

Wholewheat couscous

Wholewheat pasta

Frozen foods

Broccoli

Corn

Fruit (no sugar added)

Green beans

Peas

Spinach

Bread products

Tortillas (corn, wholewheat)

Wholegrain crispbreads

Wholemeal bread

Refrigerated foods

Butter (preferably light)

Cheese (Cheddar, Parmesan, reduced fat cream cheese, cottage)

Eggs

Reduced-fat margarine (avoid trans/hydrogenated fats)

Milk, skimmed or semi-skimmed

Orange juice

Yoghurt (low-fat bio, plain)

When shopping, always read the label!

Food labels can be very misleading, both in terms of establishing exactly how many calories you are consuming and in the terminology they use. For example, peanut butter labels may read 'cholesterol free' – this is true, but peanut butter never had cholesterol in it in the first place! And 'cholesterol free' does not mean 'fat free'. Again, some manufacturers will boast 'No Added Fat' on their 'healthy' cereal box, although in fact the contents may well have been processed with coconut or palm oil, both high in saturated fat.

Here are some things to look out for:

● Look at total fat intake and not just saturated fat. Any fat, healthy or not, provides 9 calories per gram.

● Just because it says 'low fat' on the front does not necessarily mean it is a low-fat food. An apple is a naturally low-fat food while 'low-fat' mayo is not!

● Avoid trans fats by looking for the term 'hydrogenated'. The higher up the list you see this term, the more unhealthy fats there are in the food.

● It may say 'reduced fat' on the label but do check out the total calories – the extra flavour may come by way of added sugars and processed flavourings.

Consider buying a ready-reference calorie counter or using one on-line.

Your Personal Menu Plans

Fill these in when creating your own menu plans

My daily calorie target   Day: 1 2 3 4 5 6 7

Breakfast calorie target

Lunch calorie target

Dinner calorie target

Snack 1 calorie target

Snack 2 calorie target

My daily calorie target   Day: 1 2 3 4 5 6 7

Breakfast calorie target

Lunch calorie target

Dinner calorie target

Snack 1 calorie target

Snack 2 calorie target

And now, the Recipes.
There is a whole host of flavours, textures and taste sensations for you to enjoy.

The nutritional information is given per serving for each dish. Always check how many people the recipe serves and divide the dish to get the correct portion size.

Breakfasts

Pinhead oatmeal porridge with raisins

calories 414 **fat** 7.97 **protein** 13.21 **carbohydrates** 75.04

Oatmeal is full of slow-release carbohydrates to keep you going until lunchtime. If you can't find pinhead oatmeal, use regular rolled oats and don't worry about soaking them. The recipe below is designed to be easy to fit around your morning routine, and to save on washing up.

Serves 1 Prep time: 1 minute, plus 15 minutes soaking
Cooking time: 4–5 minutes cooking
90g pinhead oatmeal
30g raisins
275ml boiling water

1 As you stumble blearily down to make a cup of tea, measure the oatmeal and raisins into a microwaveable bowl. When the kettle has boiled, pour the boiling water over the oatmeal-raisin mix and leave to soak. Go and get dressed.

2 When you're ready for breakfast, cover the bowl with cling-film and microwave on high for 3 minutes. Stir, microwave for another 1½ minutes on high and then leave to stand for 3 minutes.

3 Serve with soya milk or semi-skimmed milk.

Moosewood sesame citrus delight

calories 116.75 **fat** 2.76 **protein** 5.85 **carbohydrates** 18.24

Moosewood is a famous American vegetarian restaurant, well known for its world food and innovative cooking. This is adapted from one of its recipes.

Serves 4 Prep time: 3 minutes Chilling time: 30 minutes
400g low-fat natural yoghurt
1 tbsp toasted sesame seeds
2 tbsp honey
1 tsp freshly grated organic orange peel
1 tsp freshly grated organic lemon peel
a pinch of salt
100g berries, e.g. strawberries or raspberries, to serve

1 Toast the sesame seeds on an un-oiled baking tray in a medium oven for 2–3 minutes. Cool, then combine all of the ingredients in a bowl, cover and chill for at least half an hour.

2 Serve topped with 100g of your favourite berries.

Banana muffins

calories 337.33 **fat** 7.50 **protein** 10.12 **carbohydrates** 61.52

A weekend treat when you feel like putting a little more time into preparing brunch. Two muffins, a little non-sugar fruit jam, a glass of prune juice and herbal tea makes a 400 kcal breakfast.

Serves 6 (makes 12 muffins)
Prep time: 15 minutes Cooking time: 25 minutes
200g unbleached white flour
1/2 tsp bicarbonate of soda
1 tsp baking powder
1/2 tsp ground cinnamon
1/2 tsp nutmeg
60g brown sugar
100g porridge oats
1 egg white
1 egg
2 tbsp sunflower oil
2 ripe bananas, mashed
50g low fat natural yoghurt
50g sultanas

1 Preheat the oven to 200°C/400°F/Gas Mark 6. Prepare a muffin tin with paper liners, cooking spray or a fine coat of oil.

2 Sift together the flour, bicarbonate, baking powder and spices and stir in the sugar. Process the oats in a blender and stir into the other dry ingredients. Beat the egg white for 3 minutes until increased in volume but not stiff. Stir in the egg, oil, bananas, yoghurt and sultanas. Fold the wet ingredients into the dry until just combined but not too homogeneous.

3 Spoon the batter into the muffin tin, and bake for 20–25 minutes until a skewer comes out clean (a length of spaghetti works just as well for testing). Allow to cool in the tin for 5 minutes, then turn out onto a cooling rack.

Date and pumpkin-seed brunch loaf

calories 422 **fat** 13.56 **protein** 6.5 **carbohydrates** 72.68

This is delicious with a cup of herbal tea in the morning, with the dates and pumpkin seeds giving you fibre and lots of minerals to set you up for the day. It also freezes well, so slice it when it has cooled, layer the slices with baking parchment and wrap in a plastic bag so you can remove a single slice at a time.

Serves 8 Prep time: 15 minutes Cooking time: 25 minutes
200g fresh dates, stoned and roughly chopped
150g raisins
65g pumpkin seeds
225g self-raising flour
100g soft margarine
100g caster sugar
2 large eggs
125ml water (at room temperature)

1 Preheat the oven to 180°C/350°F/Gas Mark 4. Grease a 1lb loaf tin well. Put the dates and the raisins in a mixing bowl. In the saucepan, toast the pumpkin seeds over a medium heat (with no oil) until they begin to brown. Tip them over the dates and raisins. Sift the flour over this and mix well, to make sure that all the sticky bits of date are coated in flour.

2 Beat the margarine and sugar together, on a high speed, until the mixture is light and fluffy. Add the eggs and beat again. Add the flour/fruit mixture to the margarine/sugar mixture, pour the hot water over the top and mix with a wooden spoon until everything is incorporated.

3 Scrape into the prepared tin, level the top and bake for an hour. Check it after half an hour and put a layer of tin foil loosely over the top if it's browning too fast. A skewer inserted into the middle of the loaf should come out clean when it's ready. Remove it from the oven and leave it to cool down before tipping it out of the tin.

Low-fat natural yoghurt with granola and apple purée

calories 378   **fat** 14.35   **protein** 12.86   **carbohydrates** 54.59

Delicious, and so good for you. Serve with a cup of refreshing unsweetened herbal tea – lemon verbena is a good choice.

Serves 1 Prep time: 1 minute Cooking time: 5 minutes
1 medium eating apple, grated or sliced
100g low fat natural probiotic yoghurt
50g unsweetened muesli or granola

1 Stew the apple gently with a dessertspoon of water for 5 minutes until soft.

2 Sprinkle the yoghurt with the muesli or granola, and top with the stewed apple.

Blueberry-yoghurt slush with granola

calories 412   **fat** 14.49   **protein** 13.08   **carbohydrates** 63.01

If you can find fresh blueberries by all means use them, but the frozen ones work just as well – if not better – for this wonderfully purple breakfast.

Serves 1 Prep time: 1 minute Cooking time: none
100g low-fat natural probiotic yoghurt
100g fresh or frozen blueberries
50g muesli or granola
1 tbsp clear honey

1 Mix the yoghurt and blueberries together with a fork – how much you mix depends on how purple you like your food! Frozen blueberries will defrost as you mix them, but you might want to set the slush aside for a few minutes so you don't end up eating miniature ice cubes.

2 Place the slush in a serving bowl, top with the granola or muesli, and drizzle the honey over the top.

Poached egg on Marmite toast with freshly squeezed orange juice

calories 227   **fat** 5.39   **protein** 8.94   **carbohydrates** 37.73

A classic. If you don't like Marmite or Vegemite then add a sprinkle of salt, and be generous with the pepper grinder. You can use a poacher for the egg, but this is the real way to do it.

Serves 1 Prep time: none Cooking time: 5 minutes
1 fresh hen's egg
1 slice brown bread
1 teaspoon Marmite or Vegemite (optional)
black pepper
200ml freshly squeezed orange juice, to serve

1 Bring a little water to simmering point in a small saucepan. Break the egg into a saucer, and put the bread in the toaster. Slide the egg gently off the saucer into the simmering water – don't allow the water to boil. Note the time: the egg should be done in 2 minutes.

2 Spread the Marmite or Vegemite, if using, on the toast. Remove the egg from the water with a slotted spoon, place it on the toast and add a few grindings of pepper. Serve with a glass of freshly squeezed orange juice.

Quick breakfasts – all serve 1

Peanut butter toast

calories 349   **fat** 10.65   **protein** 10.24   **carbohydrates** 58.65

Two slices wholegrain seeded toast with 2 teaspoons peanut butter, a small sliced banana, and a 125ml glass of any natural fruit juice.

Fruity English muffin

calories 282   **fat** 6.31   **protein** 19.38   **carbohydrates** 36.69

Spread a toasted English muffin with 100g low-fat cream cheese and top with a sliced plum and a sprinkle of cinnamon.

Raspberry smoothie

calories 236   **fat** 7.79   **protein** 14.06   **carbohydrates** 31.85

Mix 1 teacup unsweetened soya or skimmed milk, 100g frozen or fresh raspberries (no added sugar), 1/2 banana, 1/2 cup silken tofu (you will find this at a health food shop in the chilled cabinet). Blend and go!

Breakfast on the go

calories 258   **fat** 12.45   **protein** 11.01   **carbohydrates** 28.92

Grab an apple (or fruit of your choice), 125g natural plain bio yoghurt and 20g nuts such as almonds or hazelnuts.

Cereal with milk

calories 260   **fat** 1.79   **protein** 12.79   **carbohydrates** 57.92

Bowl of 50g of your favourite wholewheat cereal sprinkled with a tablespoon wheatgerm, a teaspoon of crushed flaxseed and 50g blueberries, finished with ice-cold skimmed milk.

Or what about ...

A large bowl of fresh fruit salad with 100g natural low-fat bio yoghurt (215 calories)

A large slice of melon with 50g Bran Flakes, a slice of wholemeal toast with peanut butter and 275ml skimmed milk (410 calories)

A slice of orange, 2 slices of toast with 1 tsp healthy margarine and honey, and 25g Edam cheese (368 calories)

200ml orange juice, 50g Shreddies or other wholewheat cereal, a sliced banana, 1 slice toast, 1 tsp healthy margarine with 275ml skimmed milk (500 calories)

1 poached egg and grilled tomato, 50g poached mushrooms in 1 tbsp milk and a slice wholemeal toast (165 calories)

25g porridge soaked in 275ml skimmed milk, a grated apple and a handful of raisins with a pinch of cinnamon (323 calories)

A mango and banana smoothie (1 banana, 1 mango, 1/2 pot natural low-fat bio yoghurt, 275ml skimmed milk and ice) (280 calories)

Lunches

Grilled teriyaki tofu with roasted red peppers and houmous roll-up

calories 240.50   **fat** 7.94   **protein** 11.40   **carbohydrates** 37.84

This is an ideal light lunch, and if you make the Teriyaki chicken (see page 144) the night before, you'll have plenty of sauce left over for this. Cover any leftover tofu in water and store it in the fridge: as long as you change the water every 24 hours it will keep for three days or so.

Serves 2 Prep time: 2 minutes Cooking time: 5 minutes
125g firm tofu
2 tbsp teriyaki sauce
50g roasted red pepper in a jar, well drained of its oil and
*   thinly sliced*
2 tbsp houmous
2 leaves fresh, cleaned and dried Boston or roundhead
*   lettuce (or 2 leaves Romaine, shredded)*
2 wholewheat tortillas

1 Cut the tofu into four generous centimetre-thick slices. Cover with teriyaki sauce, turning gently to ensure that all sides are coated. Turn the grill to high.

2 Place a sheet of tinfoil over your grillpan (tofu can fall apart when you move it). Lay the tofu slices at least 3cm apart from each other and then place under the grill. Leave them for 3 minutes then baste with any remaining marinade; turn them over, baste again and gril for another 2 minutes. It should take about 5 minutes in total, until they are soft.

3 While the tofu is grilling, place the tortillas in the oven beneath it, to catch the residual heat from the grill and soften them. When the tofu is cooked, take the tortillas out of the oven and spread the houmous thinly over them. Lay the lettuce on top of the houmous, put the red pepper and grilled tofu on top of that and roll up tightly.

Tuna, mushroom, parsley and lemon stuffed pitta

calories 327.50   **fat** 5.19   **protein** 31.95   **carbohydrates** 37.50

This is the quick and easy 'cheat's version' of the more time-consuming Marinated tuna steak with mushrooms recipe on page 138.

Serves 2 Prep time: 5 minutes Cooking time: none
1 x 185g tin tuna in spring water, drained
200g thinly sliced button mushrooms
1/2 tbsp olive oil
100g flat-leaved parsley
juice of two lemons
salt and pepper
2 pitta bread

1 Flake the tuna into a bowl and break it up with a fork. Mix in the mushrooms, olive oil, parsley and lemon juice and add salt and pepper to taste.

2 Toast the pitta bread until it puffs up, then stuff it with the salad. Delicious.

Spicy fruity coleslaw with ham, in pitta bread

calories 333.33 **fat** 4.68 **protein** 16.30 **carbohydrates** 61.31

Coleslaw can be both incredibly bland and far too vinegary, but here's a recipe to really make your tastebuds sit up. You can adjust the amounts of all the ingredients to suit your taste, but remember that it improves with time so don't make it too spicy or fruity to start with.

Serves 6 Prep time: 15 minutes Soaking time: at least 1 hour
125g dried apricots, roughly chopped
125g seedless sultanas
1 tsp brown sugar
1 tbsp white wine vinegar
125ml apple juice
125ml orange juice
1 tsp groundnut or sunflower oil
1 large head firm white cabbage
1 tsp salt
2.5cm fresh ginger, peeled and grated or finely chopped
1 small red onion, finely diced
1/2 red chilli (optional)

1 slice cooked ham per person
1 pitta bread per person
a few leaves of fresh coriander, chopped

1 Put the chopped apricots and sultanas into the mixing bowl and add the brown sugar. Pour over the vinegar, apple and orange juices and oil and stir well. Leave to soak for up to an hour, so the fruit plumps up and absorbs the other tastes. If you don't have the time, don't worry about it, but be prepared for slightly chewy fruit in the final dish.

2 Shred the cabbage as finely as you can and add it to the fruit along with the salt, ginger and red onion. If you're using the chilli then halve it lengthways and take the seeds out with a teaspoon before shredding it thinly and tossing it gently with the rest of the mixture. Leave the coleslaw in the fridge for as long as you can, for the flavours to develop.

3 When you want to eat, toast a pitta bread until it puffs up. Cut open the long end, lay a slice of ham inside, and fill with a portion of coleslaw. Sprinkle over the fresh coriander.

Lentil salad with lardons

calories 245 **fat** 2.61 **protein** 22.43 **carbohydrates** 33.62

Another simple, nourishing and tasty lunchtime meal, which you could eat with toasted pitta bread or a wholemeal roll.

Serves 1 Prep time: 2 minutes Cooking time: 6 minutes
50g lardons or cubed pancetta
100g cherry tomatoes
1 x 125g tin Puy lentils, drained
1 tbsp finely chopped parsley
1 tbsp balsamic vinegar

1 Grill the lardons or pancetta until crisp, then drain on kitchen paper and set aside.

2 Halve the cherry tomatoes, and mix with the lentils, parsley and vinegar. Put onto a serving plate and top with the lardons.

Grilled herring on oatmeal

calories 336.50   **fat** 17.93   **protein** 34.33   **carbohydrates** 12.0

This is a healthy classic but so simple and delicious. Oatmeal is very high in fibre and iron and blends perfectly with the sweet, crunchy apple and peppery watercress salad. There's a picture of this dish on page 136.

Serves 2 Prep time: 2 minutes Cooking time: 10 minutes
2 herring, cleaned and butterflied (ask your fishmonger)
oatmeal coating
sea salt and black pepper
1 lemon

For the salad
1 apple, sliced
100g (about 4 handfuls) watercress

1 Preheat the grill to medium and line the grill rack with a sheet of foil. Wipe or rinse the herring under cold water and pat dry with kitchen paper. Season the flesh with salt and pepper and sprinkle with lemon juice. Press the herring into a plate of oatmeal until well coated and grill flesh-side up for about 10 minutes, until golden.

2 Serve with lemon wedges for squeezing, and an apple and watercress salad on the side.

Trout baked in newspaper, with flaked almonds and watercress salad

calories 344   **fat** 4.08   **protein** 8.88   **carbohydrates** 32.60

Trout and flaked almonds is a traditional combination of flavours, and the colours look magnificent on the plate.

Serves 2 Prep time: 5 minutes Cooking time: 25 minutes
2 trout, gutted but unwashed (the newspaper sticks better this way)
2 sheets tabloid-sized newspaper
120g bag watercress, or rocket/spinach/watercress salad
20g butter
2 tbsp olive oil
30g flaked almonds
1 juicy lemon
sea salt and black pepper to taste

1 Preheat the oven to 180°C/350°F/Gas Mark 4. Tip each trout onto a sheet of newspaper and wrap it up into a neat parcel, tucking the edges underneath. Place the parcels on a baking tray and bake for 25 minutes (or 20 minutes if the trout are quite small).

2 While the trout are cooking, wash the watercress and place it in a salad bowl. When the trout are almost done, melt the oil and butter in a heavy-based saucepan and fry the almonds until they are a golden brown. Remove the almonds from the oil (keep the oil) and toss them with the green salad, adding the juice of half the lemon, a pinch of salt and a few grindings of pepper.

3 When the trout are done, peel away the newspaper carefully (the trout skin sticks to it) to leave a perfectly skinned trout on each plate. Pour the oil from frying the almonds over the trout, then slice the rest of the lemon thinly and arrange the slices decoratively. Serve with the almond-speckled green salad on the side.

Italian-style mackerel with a tomato, anchovy and pea sauce

calories 464.5   **fat** 26.8   **protein** 28.3   **carbohydrates** 22.48

Unlike white fish, which store their rich, 'good' oil in their livers, the oil of fish like mackerel, herrings, sardines and pilchards is distributed throughout their bodies and makes them an ideal choice for healthy eating. Adding peas to the tomato sauce is an Italian classic and also gives you a portion of fibre- and vitamin-rich vegetables. See the photo on page 137.

Serves 2 Prep time: 10 minutes Cooking time: 12 minutes

For the fish
2 medium mackerel fillets
olive oil spray
1–2 fresh lemons

For the sauce
3 tsp olive oil
2 plump cloves garlic, peeled and finely chopped
60g black olives, pitted and finely chopped
1 tbsp parsley, finely chopped
3–4 anchovy fillets (50g), roughly chopped
1 glass red wine
230g tin chopped plum tomatoes
2 tbsp passata
lemon juice
sea salt and black pepper
150g frozen peas
3 tsp capers (optional)
good handful basil leaves, ripped

Sea salt and freshly ground black pepper

1 To make the sauce, warm the olive oil in a medium-sized pan on a low heat. Gently cook the garlic, olives and parsley without browning. Add the anchovy fillets and stir in for about a minute. Turn the heat up to medium and add the wine; stir and let it simmer for about 2 minutes. Mix in the tomatoes and the passata, simmering and stirring for 4–5 minutes or longer on a low heat, to intensify the flavours. Taste and season up as you go, with a good squeeze of lemon juice and black pepper.

2 While the sauce is cooking, pre-heat a griddle pan and lightly spray with olive oil. Rinse the mackerel fillet under a cold tap and pat dry with kitchen paper. Season the fish with a little sea salt and a good squeeze of lemon and spray the skin lightly with olive oil. Sear the fish on the hot griddle pan for about 45 seconds on each side. Turn the heat down to medium and cook for about 3 minutes on each side. To check if it is cooked, gently slide the tip of a knife along the back-bone to see if the flesh is opaque and firm.

3 Add the peas to the tomato sauce, letting them melt into the sauce for 30 seconds or so, then add the capers, if using. Stir in half of the ripped basil leaves and spoon a generous pool of sauce onto 2 warmed plates. Perch the mackerel on top with a twist of lemon and the reserved basil leaves.

Gourmet suggestions
For added flavour, pre-roast some fresh cherry or plum tomatoes on the vine, then chop and substitute for the tinned tomatoes in the sauce.

When griddling, sear thick wedges of lemon or lime alongside the fish for a great-tasting accompaniment.

Marinated tuna steak with mushroom, parsley and lemon juice salad

calories 224   **fat** 8.47   **protein** 27.98   **carbohydrates** 11.75

Fresh tuna is increasingly easy to buy and it is a delicious fish, especially when marinated as it is here. This is another dish that you can prepare in advance: it only takes a very few minutes at the grill to finish it off.

Serves 2 Prep time: 30 minutes Cooking time: 10 minutes
2 x 100g tuna steaks
2 tbsp lime juice
1 tbsp olive oil
200g thinly sliced button mushrooms
100g flat leaved parsley, finely chopped
juice of two lemons
sea salt and black pepper

1 Place the tuna steaks in a bowl with the lime juice and half of the olive oil. Turn them so that they are coated and set them aside for at least half an hour.

2 Mix the mushroom slices, parsley, lemon juice, the remaining olive oil, salt and pepper, and cover with cling film. Set aside for the flavours to mingle.

3 When you are ready to eat, preheat the grill to high. Grill the tuna steaks for 5 minutes on each side, pouring any marinade over them as you turn them over. Serve with the mushroom salad.

Caesar salad with Cajun grilled chicken

calories 336   **fat** 19.75   **protein** 35.6   **carbohydrates** 2.8

A non-traditional Caesar salad, but with a great flavour. There are several different brands of Caesar salad dressing available in the shops: taste it before serving, as you may like to jazz it up with a squeeze of lemon juice, half a teaspoon of mustard or half a teaspoon of soy sauce (or all three).

Serves 2 Prep time: 5 minutes Cooking time: 10 minutes
For the chicken
2 tbsp Cajun seasoning
1 tsp oil
2 x 100g skinless chicken breasts, cut into bite-sized chunks

For the salad
15g freshly grated Parmesan cheese
4 tbsp Caesar salad dressing
1 tsp lemon juice (optional)
1/2 tsp mustard (optional)
1/2 tsp soy sauce (optional)
100g cos lettuce leaves torn into bite-size chunks

1 Mix the oil and Cajun seasoning together in a large bowl, then add the chicken and turn with a wooden spoon until all the pieces are well coated. Leave to marinate while you wash the lettuce and adjust the Caesar salad dressing to taste.

2 Put a ridged grill pan over a high heat. Add the chicken pieces, pressing them down with a spatula for a few seconds before turning them over and pressing down again. When they're cooked take them off the heat and leave to cool.

3 Toss the lettuce leaves in the dressing and distribute them between the plates. Sprinkle the Parmesan on top and add the grilled chicken pieces with a twist of fresh black pepper.

Smoked duck breast salad with griottines

calories 213   **fat** 9.15   **protein** 10.66   **carbohydrates** 10.65

An elegant weekend lunch for two. If you like, you can serve it with a slice of wholemeal bread to soak up the juices.

Serves 2 Prep time: 5 minutes Cooking time: none

1 smoked duck breast, fat trimmed off, sliced very thinly
150g bag mixed salad, including peppery leaves like mustard, watercress or mizuna
1 tbsp griottines (morello cherries bottled in brandy)
1 tbsp liquor from the cherries
1 tbsp olive oil
sea salt and black pepper

1 Arrange a mound of leaves in the centre of each plate, with the thinly sliced duck breast and cherries around the salad.

2 Combine the cherry liquor with the olive oil and sprinkle over the salad. Season and serve; a small glass of red wine goes down very nicely indeed with this.

Quick Lunches - all serve 1

Pitta Niçoise salad

calories 366   **fat** 16.15   **protein** 35.25   **carbohydrates** 18.76

Chop 1 hard-boiled egg and 2 egg whites. Blend in a small (100g) tin salmon (packed in water) with 1 small chopped onion, 1 tbsp light mayonnaise, 1 tbsp mustard, and freshly ground black pepper (to taste). Cut the top off a wholewheat pitta, then stuff with the egg and salmon mixture, salad leaves and tomato slices.

Easy tuna melt

calories 385   **fat** 9.77   **protein** 36.78   **carbohydrates** 36.12

Mix a small (100g) can of tuna (packed in water) with 2 tbsp light mayo and one grated carrot. Divide the mixture between 2 wholewheat English muffin halves. Top each with 25g low-fat Edam cheese. Grill until the cheese bubbles.

Open sandwich

calories 214.8   **fat** 10.87   **protein** 16.62   **carbohydrates** 14.37

Spread 2 tbsp natural organic yoghurt mixed with $1/2$ tbsp fresh chopped dill and parsley on a thick slice of rye bread. Top with a 60g slice of smoked trout and garnish with side salad and 2 tsp olive oil and vinegar dressing.

Avocado and chicken wrap

calories 386   **fat** 14.29   **protein** 32.14   **carbohydrates** 31.95

Lay 100g sliced chicken breast on an open flour tortilla, top with a layer of sliced tomato, sliced avocado, a few spinach leaves and 1 tbsp salsa. Roll and go.

Lunch on the run

calories 383   **fat** 12.18   **protein** 14.07   **carbohydrates** 68.47

Grab a 90g bag of vegetable crudités, 100g pot of low-fat houmous and a small 77g wholemeal roll.

or what about...

A sliced chicken sandwich made with wholemeal bread, 1 tsp healthy spread, tomato and watercress, accompanied by a tossed green salad with oil and vinegar (1 tsp oil to 3 tsp vinegar) (370 calories)

50g Gouda cheese, a crusty wholemeal roll, carrot and celery sticks and 200ml apple juice (443 calories)

A tuna salad made with a 100g tin of tuna (packed in mineral water) mixed with a stick of diced celery, 1 tbsp chopped spring onions, a sprinkling of dill, 1 tsp low-fat natural yoghurt and 1 tsp low-fat mayonnaise, with 85g sliced cucumber and a large pear (333 calories)

300ml V8 juice, crudités of cherry tomatoes, sliced cucumber, celery and carrot sticks, 100g low-fat houmous dip (350 calories)

$^1/_2$ carton of fresh onion soup (such as New Covent Garden), with a slice of German rye bread spread with $^1/_2$ tsp healthy spread and Marmite, and 140ml glass orange juice (204 calories)

If you're buying lunch out, go for any sandwich, salad or sushi box that contains less than 350 calories. Avoid coleslaw and other salads made with mayonnaise (which can have up to 100 calories per 50g). Opt instead for an undressed tomato and onion salad or a mixed pepper salad (only 20 calories each).

Dinners

Thai green curry with beef or chicken and vegetables

calories 457.5   **fat** 26.66   **protein** 24.31   **carbohydrates** 38.84

You can buy ready-made green curry sauce, but it is so much nicer when it is fresh. This may look complicated, but if you prepare all the ingredients beforehand it is actually extremely easy and is well worth the effort.

Serves 4   Prep time: 5 minutes   Cooking time: 15 minutes

1 x 410g tin low-fat coconut milk
3 tbsp Thai green curry paste
200g lean beef or chicken breast, thinly sliced
1 medium aubergine, cut into 2cm pieces
50g green beans, topped and tailed
1 x 410g tin baby corn, drained
1 x 410g tin of mushrooms, drained
2 tbsp brown sugar
2 tbsp fish sauce
3 kaffir lime leaves, stem removed and thinly sliced
   (or use 2 tbsp lime juice with the zest of ¹/₂ lime)
60g fresh basil leaves (set a few aside for garnish)
2 large, long chillies (1 red and 1 green for colour), sliced
   lengthwise (to garnish)

For the accompanying vegetables
2 tsp vegetable oil (not olive oil)
2 x 100g packs of mixed vegetables for stir-fry

1 In a wok, stir-fry the coconut milk for 5 minutes over a high heat. Add the green curry paste and continue to stir-fry for another 2 minutes. Add the chicken or beef pieces and cook for a minute, just until they begin to change colour. Add the aubergine pieces and continue to cook until they are just soft.

2 Now add the green beans and cook for another 2 minutes before adding the tinned mushrooms and baby corn.

3 Add the brown sugar and stir to dissolve, then add the fish sauce, kaffir lime leaves (or lime juice and zest), and basil.

4 Pour into a serving dish, quickly rinse out the wok and return it to a high heat with a teaspoon of vegetable oil.

5 Tip the vegetables into the wok and stir-fry briskly for a minute or so until they are just cooked but still retain some crunch.

6 Garnish the curry with some basil leaves and the sliced red and green chillies.

Teriyaki chicken on red onion and mushrooms, with Savoy cabbage

calories 317   **fat** 10.73   **protein** 35.78   **carbohydrates** 18.32

Teriyaki sauce is traditionally used in Japanese cooking to give a dark glaze to meat or vegetables. It is relatively easy to track down in health food shops and supermarkets, although it's easy to make yourself and keeps for weeks in the cupboard. It goes extraordinarily well with mushrooms, giving them a real depth of flavour – and the leftover sauce can be used to flavour soups or stir-fries.

Serves 2 Prep time: 10 minutes Cooking time: 25 minutes
To make your own teriyaki sauce:
150ml dark soy sauce
100ml rice mirin
1 tbsp dark muscovado sugar

For the chicken
1 tbsp olive oil
1 red onion, halved and thinly sliced
250g flat cap or Portobello mushrooms, cleaned and sliced (about 1cm thick)
2 pieces of tinfoil, about 30 x 20cm
2 x 100g skinless chicken breasts
2 tsp teriyaki sauce (see above)
100g Savoy cabbage leaves

1 To make the teriyaki sauce, place all the ingredients in a heavy-bottomed saucepan and bring to the boil, stirring gently to dissolve the sugar. Turn the heat down to medium and simmer for about 10 minutes, until the liquid has reduced by half. Cool, and store in a clean jam-jar.

2 Preheat the oven to 200°C/390°F/Gas Mark 6. Heat the olive oil in a non-stick frying pan over medium heat. Add the red onion and sliced mushrooms, and fry until the mushrooms turn dark brown and begin to give off a little liquid. Divide the mushroom-onion mixture evenly between the two pieces of tinfoil, and place a chicken breast on top of each one.

3 Rub a teaspoon of teriyaki sauce over each chicken breast, then make a parcel out of the tinfoil by bringing together its opposite edges and crimping them gently. Don't wrap it tightly or the foil will stick to the chicken; but do make the parcel as airtight as possible so that the steam can't escape. Place the parcels on a baking tray and place in the oven for 20 minutes.

4 While they are baking, trim and wash the cabbage and remove the larger ribs. Cut it into chunky pieces, place them in a microwaveable bowl with a tablespoon of water and cover the bowl with clingfilm. When the chicken is done, take it out of the oven and leave it to stand while you microwave the cabbage on high for 4 minutes. Drain the cabbage, divide it between the plates, and then open the tinfoil parcels carefully and tip the chicken, mushrooms and all the glorious juices over the top.

Chicken fillet en papillote with baked tomatoes and green beans

calories 316.50 **fat** 7.87 **protein** 40.13 **carbohydrates** 21.01

Cooking 'en papillote' (in an envelope) is a lovely way to keep the moistness and flavour in. It's particularly good for chicken.

Serves 2 Prep time: 10 minutes Cooking time: 30 minutes
2 x 100g chicken fillets
2 bay leaves
peppercorns
2 tbsp white wine
2 large tomatoes
2 tsp olive oil
a sprinkle of thyme leaves or dried thyme
200g runner beans, topped, tailed and chopped

1 Preheat the oven to 180°C/350°F/Gas Mark 4. Put each chicken fillet on a square of tin foil, place a bayleaf and a few peppercorns on top of each one, and drizzle the wine over them. Form a sealed parcel by folding the tinfoil loosely around the chicken and crimping the edges together. Place in an ovenproof dish.

2 Cut the tomatoes in half, across their width. Sprinkle them with the thyme, a pinch of salt, a few grindings of pepper, and a drizzle of olive oil. Place the tomatoes in another oven-proof dish and bake them, with the chicken, for 30 minutes.

3 Bring a pan of salted water to the boil. Simmer the beans for 5 minutes, drain and serve with the chicken and baked tomatoes.

Chilli chicken and white bean burgers with soya 'mayo'

calories 434.5   **fat** 11.4   **protein** 40.08   **carbohydrates** 45.18

Flaxseed (linseed) is an abundant source of Omega 3 and Omega 6 essential fatty acids, which are very important in our diet. It has a pleasant nutty flavour and will reduce and even replace the need for salt. Serve these flaxseed-enriched burgers my Carb Curfew way, balanced on a large, baked field mushroom 'bap' with parsnip chips on the side.

Serves 2 Prep time: 15 minutes Cooking time: 40 minutes
For the burgers
200g drained (canned) canellini beans
200g skinless chicken breast, minced or roughly chopped
75g grated courgette
75g grated carrot
4 spring onions, sliced
2 cloves garlic, finely chopped
1 red chilli, finely chopped
1 tablespoon ground flaxseed
good handful coriander, chopped
3 teaspoons olive oil
Sea salt and freshly ground black pepper
1 small egg, beaten

3 medium parsnips, peeled and sliced into chip wedges
2 large field mushrooms
3 beef tomatoes, sliced
3 beetroots, sliced

For the soya 'mayo'
5 chopped radishes
3 tbsp yofu/low fat natural yoghurt

1 Preheat the oven to 200°C/400°F/Gas Mark 6 and lightly spray a baking tray with olive oil. At the same time, line a roasting tray with tin foil and set aside.

2 Chop the parsnips into long, chip wedges and spray with olive oil. Arrange on the roasting tray and bake in the oven for 40 minutes, turning occasionally.

3 Mash the drained beans roughly and then purée half of them to a smooth texture. In a large bowl, combine the beans with the chicken, courgette, carrot, spring onions, garlic, chilli, flaxseed, coriander, olive oil and seasoning, using your hands to thoroughly mould the mixture together. Carefully add just enough beaten egg so that the mixture holds together, without being too soft.

4 Divide the burger mix into 4 pattie shapes and place on the baking tray. Bake in the oven for about 30 minutes, without turning them. Halfway through cooking, drizzle a teaspoon of olive oil on top of each mushroom and add them to the tray.

5 Mix the radishes with 3 tablespoons yofu and season to taste. Balance each burger on a large mushroom and spoon over the soy 'mayo' to taste. Serve with a tomato and beetroot salad.

Tray-baked citrus chicken with lentils and rocket

calories 350.33   **fat** 10.55   **protein** 31.69   **carbohydrates** 33.49

This is great for a dinner party as there is so little to do, but it has so much flavour and it also looks tasty (see page 148). You can leave the chicken to marinate all day if you want to, but if you do you must be sure to bring the dish to room temperature before you begin cooking it.

Serves 6 Prep time: 5 minutes Cooking time: 45 minutes
8 chicken thighs
l unwaxed lemon
2 oranges
125ml chicken stock (fresh, if you can find it)
2 tbsp balsamic vinegar
4 sprigs rosemary
¹/₂ tsp sea salt
a few grindings of black pepper
2 x 410g tins of cooked lentils, drained
2 x 100g bags rocket, or spinach/rocket/watercress salad
1 tbsp olive oil

1 Preheat the oven to 180°C/350°F/Gas Mark 4. Cut the oranges and lemon into quarters, and squeeze some of the juice into a small bowl. Add the chicken stock, balsamic vinegar, salt and pepper, and mix well.

2 Cut each citrus piece in half again. Arrange the chicken pieces in a large baking dish: they shouldn't overlap. Tuck the orange, half of the lemon pieces, and three of the rosemary sprigs in between the chicken thighs (reserve the remaining pieces of lemon).

3 Pour over the citrus/stock mixture, cover with tin foil and place in the centre of the oven for 20 minutes. Remove the foil, baste the chicken pieces with the juice that's collected in the bottom of the dish; then turn the heat up to 200°C/390°F/Gas Mark 6 and cook for another 20 minutes to brown the chicken.

4 When the chicken is done (when pierced with a skewer, the juices should run clear), turn off the oven, remove the chicken and gently squash the citrus pieces to release a little more juice (but don't mash them). Carefully pour or ladle all the juices into a saucepan. Re-cover the chicken with the tinfoil and leave it to rest in the oven with the door ajar.

5 Boil the chicken juices vigorously for a few minutes, then tip the lentils into the pan with the remaining sprig of rosemary and warm them through, checking the seasoning. Serve with the green salad, dressed with a little olive oil, salt and pepper, and the juice squeezed from the reserved lemon pieces.

Beetroot, butternut squash, fennel and carrot with soy-marinated tofu

calories 209.5   **fat** 5.61   **protein** 8.57   **carbohydrates** 34.41

This colourful autumnal mix of roasted vegetables (see page 149) is great for taste and texture and also full of vitamins and anti-oxidant properties. Tofu is also one of the best sources of plant hormones and provides essential fatty acids. Feel free to choose your vegetables according to seasonal availability and personal taste. It doesn't matter if they don't all roast to uniform tenderness – a bit of crunchiness is nice!

Serves 2 Prep time: 15 minutes Cooking time: 30–40 minutes

4 beetroot, cooked, peeled and quartered

1 medium-sized butternut squash, chopped into fairly large chunks

2 fennel bulbs, trimmed, halved and par-boiled

a bunch of young carrots, cut into strips

1 large red onion, cut into 6 wedges

2 cloves of garlic, unpeeled

3 tbsp olive oil, or use olive oil spray

sea salt and freshly ground black pepper

1 tbsp herbed or spiced ground flaxseed seasoning (optional)

For the tofu

125g plain tofu, cut into bite-sized cubes

2–3 tbsp soy sauce

hot chilli sauce (optional)

To finish

a good handful of chopped parsley or coriander

dish of pickled chillies

low-fat yoghurt, cream cheese or yofu alternative, for dolloping

wedges of lemon for squeezing

1 Preheat the oven to 200°C/400°F/Gas Mark 6. Spray a roasting tin with olive oil to cover. While the oven is heating up, you can par-boil the firmer vegetables for 3 minutes if you don't want them too crunchy.

2 Spray all the vegetables with olive oil or toss in 2–3 tablespoons of olive oil. Season well and then wedge in the unpeeled cloves of garlic. Roast for 30–40 minutes, turning the vegetables once during cooking. If they need a bit longer, turn the oven down to a medium heat and cook for a further 10 to 15 minutes.

3 While the vegetables are roasting, marinate the tofu cubes in a spoonful or two of soy sauce for at least half an hour – a bit longer won't hurt. Heat up a wok or frying pan, spray with oil and sauté the tofu, tossing repeatedly until it begins to get crispy in places – then dash in a drop more soy, or a splash of hot chilli sauce.

4 Dish the roasted vegetables onto warmed plates. Squeeze the sweet garlic purée from the skins into the hot pan to mix with the tofu and then tip over the vegetables. Sprinkle with lots of chopped herbs and serve immediately with the pickled chillies, yoghurt and lemon wedges.

Serving suggestion
The roasted vegetables could be served inside a baby squash, which has been baked in the oven with herbs for 40 minutes and then rubbed with garlic purée.

Mexican vegetable soup

calories 248   **fat** 3.22   **protein** 13.24   **carbohydrates** 44.4

This is extremely easy to make, freezes well, and has a lovely smoky flavour. The refried beans add both protein and thickening to the soup; if you can't find them, then use an extra can of pinto or cannellini beans instead, mashing them up with a fork before you put them into the pot. Eat the soup as soon as possible after it's prepared, so that you don't lose the vibrant green colour of the French beans. If you like your soup hot and spicy, you can use bottled salsa, but I prefer it with the fresh tomato taste.

Serves 4 Prep time: 10 minutes Cooking time: 15 minutes

1 tsp olive oil

1 medium red onion, finely chopped

2 cloves garlic, finely chopped

1/2 tsp ground coriander

2 medium carrots, peeled and cut into bite-sized chunks

1.25 litres vegetable stock (or 1.25 litres water and two
vegetable stock cubes)

1 x 415g tin refried beans

1 x 415g tin cannellini beans

1/2 tsp dried oregano

1 tbsp chopped jalapeno chillies (from a jar)

350g green French beans, topped, tailed and cut into
bite-sized chunks

juice of 1/2 a lime

For the tomato salsa

2 medium tomatoes,

1 spring onion, thinly sliced

30g (a small bunch) fresh coriander, finely chopped

juice of 1/2 a lime

1/2 tsp salt

1 Mix together the ingredients for the salsa and set aside.

2 Use a heavy-bottomed pan to fry the onions in the oil over a medium heat. When they are translucent, add the garlic and ground coriander and fry for a minute more. Add the carrots, vegetable stock, refried beans, cannellini beans and dried oregano and bring gently to the boil, stirring fairly regularly. Simmer for 5 minutes, then add the jalapeno chillies, French beans and lime juice. Simmer for another 3 minutes, check for salt and then serve, putting a good dollop of the tomato salsa in the middle of each bowl.

3 If you want to freeze the leftovers, add any remaining salsa to the soup beforehand and as you reheat the soup you can refresh the taste with a little more lime juice and chopped fresh coriander.

Asian-flavoured sweetcorn chowder

calories 108   **fat** 3.22   **protein** 5.29   **carbohydrates** 17.39

A traditional chowder is a soup made with milk; here I use silken tofu to give the same creaminess, but without the fat. You can find silken tofu in health food shops; it is very versatile, absorbs flavours without changing them, and is full of goodness. Add some to your morning smoothie for an early protein hit.

Serves 4 Prep time: none Cooking time: 15 minutes
300ml vegetable stock (use fresh stock, not a stock cube)
600ml water
1 tsp ginger purée
1/2 tsp sea salt
300g canned sweetcorn, drained
200g silken tofu
juice of half a lime
1/2 tsp toasted sesame oil
2 spring onions (green and white parts), thinly sliced

1 Put the stock, water, ginger purée, salt and two-thirds of the sweetcorn into a pan. Bring to the boil and simmer gently for 10 minutes.

2 Remove from the heat, add the silken tofu and blend until fairly smooth. Add the rest of the sweetcorn and simmer for another 3 minutes. Add the lime juice, stir it in and check for salt and to see if you need to add more lime juice.

3 Ladle into bowls, then sprinkle a few drops of sesame oil and the spring onions on top.

Gazpacho

calories 95   **fat** 7.15   **protein** 1.28   **carbohydrates** 6.88

A light soup that's a doddle to make and that benefits from being left in the fridge for a few hours. Makes a good starter for a dinner party.

Serves 2 Prep time: 15 minutes Cooking time: none
200g ripe tomatoes
quarter of a cucumber, peeled and chopped
2 spring onions, peeled and chopped
half a red pepper
1 clove garlic
1 tbsp olive oil
1/2 tbsp wine vinegar
1 heaped tsp fresh chopped herbs, according to
   season
150ml cold water
salt and pepper
Tabasco sauce (optional)

1 Pour boiling water over the tomatoes to cover them. After a minute or two remove them and peel off the skins. Halve the tomatoes and remove the seeds.

2 Combine the peeled tomatoes with all the rest of the ingredients and blend in a food processor. Season to taste and place in the fridge to chill. Add a dash of Tabasco sauce if you like it hot.

Thai vegetable soup

calories 226.50   fat 1.05   protein 9.5   carbohydrates 15.25

This is a deliciously light soup, full of Eastern flavour. If you can't find kaffir lime leaves, add an extra squeeze of lime juice.

Serves 2 Prep time: 10 minutes Cooking time: 10 minutes

1.5 litres vegetable stock

4 cloves of garlic, crushed and chopped

4 shallots, sliced

2 stalks lemongrass, very thinly sliced
   (discarding the root end)

2¹/2cm piece of ginger, chopped finely, or 1 tsp ginger
   purée

2 tbsp Thai fish sauce

4 kaffir lime leaves, deveined and sliced thinly
   (optional)

2 tbsp lime juice

50g baby corn, sliced into rings

50g green beans, topped, tailed and cut in half

1 medium carrot, thinly sliced

200g oyster or shiitake mushrooms

30g mangetouts

2 spring onions, chopped into 1cm pieces
   (use both green and white parts)

2 medium tomatoes, roughly chopped

60g fresh coriander, roughly chopped

30g fresh mint, roughly chopped

5–7 small Thai chillies or green chillies, sliced lengthwise
   (optional)

1 Place a wok or a large saucepan over a high heat. Add 250ml of stock and bring it to the boil. Add the crushed garlic, chopped shallots, lemongrass and ginger and bring back to the boil, stirring constantly.

2 Add the rest of the stock and return to the boil again before adding the fish sauce, lime leaves and lime juice. If you like it hot, add the chillies at this stage. Add the baby corn, green beans and carrot and simmer for a minute.

3 Add the mushrooms, mangetouts, spring onions and tomatoes and simmer for another 2 minutes. Incorporate the coriander and mint immediately before serving.

Chickpea, chilli and tomato soup

calories 301   fat 2.45   protein 10.83   carbohydrates 63.39

For the days when you need something hot and are in a hurry. This also freezes very well.

Serves 1 Prep time: none Cooking time: 20 minutes

1 heaped tsp chilli purée (or to taste)

1 x 410g tin chopped tomatoes in juice

150g (half a tin) chickpeas, drained

1 tbsp finely chopped fresh parsley

1 Squirt the chilli purée into a saucepan, and heat gently (stirring) until it is nicely aromatic. Add the tinned tomatoes, bring to simmering point and simmer for 15 minutes. For a smoother textured soup base, blend the tomato mixture using a wand blender.

2 Add the chickpeas and warm through. Serve in a soup bowl with a liberal sprinkling of finely chopped parsley.

Chickpea and almond crêpes with grilled courgettes and chicory

calories 422.5   **fat** 28.07   **protein** 20.49   **carbohydrates** 28.5

These high-protein, low-fat crêpes (see page 156) are highly versatile and can be used as a base for all manner of Carb Curfew, low-calorie suppers.

Serves 2 Prep time: 5 minutes Cooking time: 5 minutes
For the crêpes
110g almonds, ground
50g chickpea flour
1 tbsp flaxseed
1 egg
200ml soya milk
a pinch of sea salt
olive oil spray
water, if necessary

For the topping
2–3 medium courgettes (200g)
1 head chicory
garlic and herb flavoured olive oil
handful of parsley, chopped
handful chives, snipped
a little Parmesan, grated

To serve
1 small pack mixed beansprouts

1 Blend all the crêpe ingredients until smooth and set aside while you prepare the vegetables. Warm a plate for stacking the pancakes in a medium oven.

2 Preheat the griddle pan so that it is hot. Wipe the courgettes with dampened kitchen paper and slice lengthways into long strips, not more than 0.5cm thick. Break off leaves of chicory. Spray them with olive oil, season lightly and place on the hot griddle pan, turning from time to time until they are slightly charred.

3 While the vegetables are grilling, take the crêpe mix and if necessary add water to thin it slightly. Spray a non-stick pan with olive oil and heat to medium/hot. Pour in 1 ladle of the mixture and swirl it round the pan so that it covers the base.

4 After about 30 seconds, bubbles will form on the top and the edges will begin to set. When you see this, flip the crêpe over and cook for 30 seconds on the other side. Transfer to a warmed plate and cover while you cook the next ones.

5 To serve, dish 1 or 2 pancakes onto each plate and top with the chargrilled vegetables, some flavoured oil and a little grated Parmesan. Shower with lots of chopped parsley and chives and a beansprout salad on the side.

Aromatic summer salmon with purple grape and mango salsa

calories 292.5   **fat** 7.32   **protein** 22.17   **carbohydrates** 37.54

Steaming is an especially easy and healthy way to cook fish for it preserves the essential Omega 3 fats and makes for a very light and fresh tasting meal (see page 157). The fruity salsa is also good with grilled and marinated chicken or tofu and the red grapes will rebuild strength for tomorrow's workout!

Serves 2 Prep time: 10 minutes Cooking time: 15 minutes

For the fish

2 x 100g fillets salmon

sea salt and freshly ground black pepper

1 lemon

2 spring onions

a few shavings ginger

For the salsa

1 bunch spring onion, trimmed but including some of the green part

1 clove garlic, peeled and finely chopped

1 tbsp ginger, grated

1 mango, cubed

1 nectarine, cubed (optional)

small bunch purple grapes, halved

1 handful coriander, chopped

1 handful mint, chopped

mixed flax and sesame seeds, toasted

2 tbsp red grape juice

generous squeeze lemon juice

salad mix of baby spinach, rocket and watercress

1 Set up the steamer and put the water on to boil. Mix all the salsa ingredients together in a bowl, season to taste and then set aside for the flavours to develop while the salmon is cooking.

2 Rinse the salmon under cold running water and pat dry with kitchen paper. Season the fish with a little sea salt, freshly ground black pepper and a good squeeze of lemon juice.

3 On two sheets of lightly oiled kitchen foil, make a bed of spring onion and ginger and lay the salmon on top with a squeeze of lemon. Loosely crimp and seal the foil and then place both parcels in the steamer tray. Steam for approximately 15 minutes.

4 Arrange the salad leaves on two plates. Heap a good serving of the salsa in the middle and top with the hot, steamed aromatic salmon.

Grilled salmon steak with wilted baby spinach and mushrooms

calories 319.5   **fat** 18.39   **protein** 30.11   **carbohydrates** 12.83

Salmon is easy to get hold of now, but there are differences in the taste and fat content that depend on where the fish are cultivated. I prefer to buy fresh from the fish stall in the super-market as I can check for colour (not too orangey-pink) and for fattiness, but there are some perfectly good frozen varieties.

Serves 2 Prep time: 10 minutes Cooking time: 10 minutes
2 x 100g salmon steaks
1 tbsp olive oil
200g sliced mushrooms
500g baby spinach
sea salt and black pepper
grated nutmeg (optional)
1 lemon

1 Preheat the grill to high. Put the salmon steaks on the grill pan and grill for 5 minutes on each side.

2 As the salmon cooks, heat the oil in a large frying pan, add the mushrooms, and stir until lightly coated; then cover the pan with a lid, turn down the heat and leave to cook slowly for about 10 minutes, stirring from time to time.

3 Rinse the spinach and place it in a covered saucepan over a low to medium heat. Shake the pan from time to time to stop it sticking. It should be wilted in 5 minutes; when it is done, drain it in a colander and season with salt, pepper and a small grating of nutmeg.

4 Squirt some lemon juice, salt and pepper over the mush-rooms. Arrange the salmon steaks, spinach and mushrooms on a plate with a slice of lemon and serve.

Baked haddock fillet with spinach

calories 202.5   **fat** 9.53   **protein** 24.71   **carbohydrates** 7.0

A very simple and quick way of serving fish. If you're using frozen fillets, make sure that they're thoroughly defrosted before you begin to cook them.

Serves 2 Prep time: 3 minutes Cooking time: 10 minutes
2 x 100g haddock fillets
20g butter
two pinches of saffron
sea salt and black pepper
400g fresh spinach

1 Preheat the oven to 180°C/350°F/Gas Mark 4. Place the haddock fillets on a non-stick tray and dot them with the butter, saffron, salt and pepper. Bake for 8–10 minutes, depending on the thickness of the fish.

2 While the fish is cooking, rinse the spinach leaves and put them in a covered saucepan with a little water. Place over a low heat for about 5 minutes until it wilts.

3 Drain the spinach, season with salt and pepper and serve with the fish, pouring any cooking juices over the spinach.

Easy fish and prawn curry

calories 259.50   **fat** 2.58   **protein** 33.17   **carbohydrates** 27.5

This is an unbelievably easy way of cooking fish, but extremely tasty. It's great to throw together when you get home: it'll be ready by the time you've wound down from your day. If you are using frozen fish or prawns, make sure that they are thoroughly defrosted before you begin.

Serves 2 Prep time: 5 minutes Cooking time: 30 minutes

2 x 100g fillets skinless white fish, such as haddock, coley or cod

100g prawns

1 x 410g tin chopped tomatoes in tomato juice (tinned cherry tomatoes work very well)

125ml semi-skimmed milk

2 tbsp flour

1 tbsp curry paste

50g fresh coriander, chopped

1 Preheat the oven to 180°C/350°F/Gas Mark 4. Chop the fish into bite-sized chunks, mix with the prawns and place in a shallow baking dish.

2 Put the chopped tomatoes, milk, flour and curry paste into a bowl and stir well with a wooden spoon until there are no floury lumps at all.

3 Stir in half the chopped fresh coriander, then pour the tomato mixture over the fish and prawns. Cover the dish with tinfoil and bake for 30 minutes. Sprinkle over the rest of the fresh coriander before serving. This goes very well with peas or green beans.

Gammon steak with Puy lentils and stir-fried greens

calories 363.5   **fat** 7.86   **protein** 31.54   **carbohydrates** 47.39

Lentils have an undeservedly bad reputation: they are delicious if properly cooked and served with complementary flavours. The orange juice in this dish gives it a real lift, and goes very well with the stir-fried greens. If you're not familiar with Puy lentils, they are small and very dark green; they don't need presoaking.

Serves 2 Prep time: 5 minutes Cooking time: 20 minutes
200g Puy lentils
2 bay leaves
2 x 100g gammon steaks
juice of two oranges (blood oranges, if you can find them)
400g Savoy cabbage leaves, shredded and rinsed
2 tbsp soy sauce

1 Preheat the oven to 180°C/350°F/Gas Mark 4. Cover the lentils generously with water, add the bay leaves and bring to the boil. Simmer gently for 20 minutes.

2 Put the gammon steaks side by side in an ovenproof dish. Pour the orange juice over them and cover lightly with tin foil. Put in the oven and bake for 10 minutes.

3 While the lentils and gammon are cooking, stir-fry the cabbage with a few drops of water for a few minutes until it begins to wilt, then add the soy sauce and put the lid on. Allow to steam for a further 5–10 minutes, stirring occasionally.

4 Serve the gammon on a bed of lentils with the cooking juice poured on top, and the cabbage on the side.

Puddings

Orange, mango and passion fruit salad

calories 123.75   **fat** 0.37   **protein** 2.12   **carbohydrates** 31.56

Passion fruit give a great deal of taste for their size. Look for the purple ones that have gone all wrinkly on the outside, as they are likely to be the sweetest.

Serves 4 Prep time: 20 minutes Cooking time: 5 minutes
3 passion fruit
2 tsp honey
6 juicy sweet oranges
1 large or 2 small mangoes, good and ripe
zest of 3 of the oranges, cut into very fine strips

1 Cut the tops off the passion fruit and scoop out the insides with a teaspoon, putting them into a small saucepan.

2 Add the honey and 2 tablespoons of water, and heat gently until the orange flesh has dissolved and the black pips are floating freely (you don't have to do this, but it stops the passion fruit clumping together). Leave to cool.

3 Peel the oranges and cut off as much of the pith as you can. Use a serrated knife to cut them into thin rings then lay them in a serving dish. Cut the stone out of the mango, and peel and roughly chop the flesh. Mix this with the oranges and pour over the passion fruit – pips and syrup.

4 Sprinkle the orange zest over the top and leave in the fridge for several hours if you can, for the flavours to develop.

5 This is best served chilled but not straight from the fridge (coldness tends to kill the flavours).

Rhubarb and strawberry jelly

calories 11.25   **fat** 0.11   **protein** 0.47   **carbohydrates** 2.52

Experiment with different fruit for this easy, make-in-advance dessert. You could try fresh blueberries in a lemon jelly, poached apricots in raspberry jelly... the combinations are endless. Serve in Martini glasses, or large wine goblets, to show off the gorgeous colours.

Serves 4 Prep time: 15 minutes Cooking time: 15 minutes
Setting time: 6–8 hours
200g rhubarb
1 tbsp lemon juice
1 packet sugar-free strawberry jelly

1 Wash and slice the rhubarb into 1cm lengths. Place them in a covered saucepan with the lemon juice and cook over a gentle heat for 5–10 minutes, stirring occasionally. Strain the rhubarb, reserving the juice.

2 Make up the jelly, as per packet instructions, incorporating the rhubarb liquid in the required amount of water. Leave to cool to room temperature before carefully mixing in the cooked rhubarb, and pouring into the serving dishes.

3 Leave to set in the fridge for at least 6 hours.

Baked bananas en papillote

WITHOUT ALMONDS

calories 65.0   **fat** 0.68   **protein** 2.19   **carbohydrates** 13.51

WITH ALMONDS

calories 111.75   **fat** 4.78   **protein** 3.92   **carbohydrates** 15.11

A grown-up version of banana splits, warm and spicy.

Serves 4 Prep time: 5 minutes Cooking time: 20 minutes
4 bananas
juice of 2 oranges
2 tsp grated orange rind
2 tsp grated lemon rind
a few pinches of cinnamon
125g low-fat natural yoghurt
50g toasted slivered almonds (optional)

1 Preheat the oven to 180°C/350°F/Gas Mark 4. Place each banana in a square of foil large enough to fold up into a little tent. Add the orange juice, orange and lemon rind and cinnamon and seal each parcel with a double fold. Place the tents on a baking tray and bake for 20 minutes.

2 You can just lift the tents onto the plates and let everyone unwrap them. Serve natural yoghurt and toasted slivered almonds on the side.

Cinnamon-poached fruit

calories 143.83   **fat** 0.21   **protein** 1.07   **carbohydrates** 38.23

This works well as a cold dessert, but is also great in the morning with a dollop of low-fat yoghurt. It keeps for days in the fridge if you cover it with clingfilm. Choose your own combination of fruit, or buy 'dried fruit salad' from the health food shop.

Serves 6 Prep time: 5 minutes Cooking time: 40 minutes
250g mixed dried apple, apricot, pineapple, prunes, mango,
cherry, blueberry
2 cinnamon sticks
4 tbsp honey

1 Place the dried fruit in a large heavy-based casserole dish with the cinnamon sticks and honey. Pour in water to cover it by at least 2cm and simmer gently for 40 minutes, checking frequently to make sure that the water hasn't evaporated: you want a good amount of delicious juice to serve with it.

2 When the fruit pieces have plumped and softened, remove from the heat, leave to cool and then refrigerate. This dish benefits from being made the day in advance to allow the flavours to develop. Depending on your choice of fruit, you may want to add a little more honey before serving.

Peaches baked with mascarpone

calories 51.0 **fat** 1.67 **protein** 1.75 **carbohydrates** 7.92

Another very easy dessert. Use fresh peaches in season (wait until they are fully ripe or they tend to be tasteless) or you can use tinned peaches for this dish.

Serves 4 Prep time: 5 minutes Cooking time: 20 minutes
2 peaches
4 tsp mascarpone cheese
2 tsp granulated sugar
20g toasted almond slivers

1 Preheat the oven to 180°C/350°F/Gas Mark 4. Halve and stone the peaches and place them in an ovenproof dish, cut side up. Place a teaspoon of cheese in the hollow of each peach half, and sprinkle with half a teaspoon of sugar.

2 Cover the dish loosely with tin foil and bake for 10 minutes. Remove the tin foil and bake for another 10 minutes. Sprinkle the toasted almond slivers over each peach, and serve.

Chocolate chip banana snack cake

calories 432 **fat** 18.24 **protein** 7.05 **carbohydrates** 63.5

Who says you can't have chocolate cake when you're trying to lose weight? Here's a recipe for a delicious treat that's not *too* high in calories – because you're worth it!

Serves 8 Prep time: 10 minutes Cooking time: 25 minutes
125g butter
60g granulated sugar
60g brown sugar
2 medium eggs
2 small ripe bananas
250g flour
1/2 tsp salt
1/2 tsp baking soda
4 tbsp plain yoghurt or sour cream
1 tsp vanilla extract
185g chocolate chips
1/2 tsp cinnamon mixed with a little caster sugar

1 Preheat the oven to 180°C/350°F/Gas Mark 4, and grease and flour a 23 x 30cm baking tin. Cream the butter and sugar together until the mixture is light and fluffy (approximately 5 minutes with electric stand mixer). Add the eggs, one at a time, beating well after each addition and then the bananas, mixing well and scraping the sides.

2 Sift the dry ingredients together, and then add them to the butter and sugar mixture. Add the yoghurt (or sour cream) and vanilla, followed by the chocolate chips and mix together well to obtain a smooth batter, but do not overbeat.

3 Pour the batter into your prepared tin, and liberally sprinkle cinnamon-sugar mixture over the top of the cake. Bake for approximately 25 minutes on the middle shelf of the oven. When the cake's ready a skewer will come out clean.

6take action!

Ready, get set, go!

This is it! Here are your Action Plans. They plot out a logical, progressive and achievable way for you to reach your journey's destination. There are different plans to choose from designed to suit your own particular weight loss challenges and the pace at which you want to travel.

Time to lose some weight

You're by now fully armed with all your tools and you should have everything you need. But don't panic if things don't always go according to plan. As you know, you will come across barriers blocking your way; your body may not always respond how you would like it to; and of course there will be times when you do lapse. So as well as your Action Plans I've also included in this chapter a selection of tried and tested ways to bash down barriers, as well as some contingency plans for when you do slip. Once you have reached your weight loss destination, staying there is just as important – so you'll find consolidation plans too.

This chapter is about helping you to make this happen. You'll never be more ready than you are now, so let's get going, and feel empowered! We're off!

What you need to do

First of all, establish which weight loss goal is realistic for you, and choose the corresponding Action Plan. Each plan details, phase by phase, the appropriate diet and level of physical activity needed to create your required Energy Gap. The plans first of all focus on decreasing your body fat and weight with cardiovascular exercise and then introduce more specific toning exercises to shape and tone your new body. The menu plans also evolve according to your calorie needs – they will change, and this needs to be reflected in what you are eating. You may also find your eating preferences change naturally as you continue on your weight loss journey.

How the Action Plans work

Each Action Plan is divided into 4-week phases which have a specific theme. Each week sets out a series of achievable tasks which are progressive, helping you to realise your goals and reinforce your Template of Success. The exact specifics of what you eat and how you move your body I've left to you, so that you can make these action plans fit in with your life. Once your Action Plan is finished, there follows a 4-week consolidation phase to help establish your new habits and keep your weight where you want it to be.

Choosing the right Action Plan for you

Remember that your aim on your weight loss journey is to make lifestyle and dietary alterations that can be maintained for the long term, instead of changes that last just for a short period. A realistic target is to lose approximately 5–10 per cent of initial body weight after 6 months. You will not only look and feel much better but will be healthier as well. This level of weight loss results in significant improvements in blood pressure, insulin resistance and blood cholesterol levels, and can be achieved with moderate calorie restriction and moderate physical activity.

Being prepared

Just as you would when you start out on any journey, you need to put some time aside to get prepared and organised. Prior preparation prevents poor performance – so the saying goes, and there is a lot of truth to it. To get off on the right foot, you may be well advised to have a quick flick through all you have learned, just to refresh your memory.

I have designed the Action Plans so that you can achieve real success, and monitoring your progress is a significant part of this. Research has shown conclusively that the more information you monitor the better your weight loss will be, so in your Action Plans you will find a series of checklists to complete. They are designed to provide a support network for you, and strengthen your Template of Success.

Things to remember

● Although you may find it possible to lose substantially more weight than is stipulated, exceeding the recommended limits can cause loss of water and lean body mass. Remember that by preserving lean body mass, the body's Resting Metabolic Rate can be maintained, helping you to become a Fat Burner rather than a Fat Storer. So don't overdo it!

● Some weeks on your Action Plan you may not lose any weight at all. This can occur as your body is reassessing the food you are consuming and how you are exercising. Don't be disheartened – just carry on with the plan.

● Sometimes you may plateau because your Energy Gap isn't as large or as consistently maintained as you think it is. Make sure you remember to track your progress to keep this in check.

What to do

● Note your measurements, your goal weight and your energy needs in the Starting Line Form on page 172. The purpose of this is to record your start point and objectives as you embark on your weight loss journey.

● Decide how big an Energy Gap you want to achieve and fill this in as well.

● Select your Weight Loss Action Plan, based on the amount of weight you want to lose

● Complete the first New Phase Record Chart (see page 172) – they are for plotting your personal objectives for each new phase of your weight loss journey.

● Have your Menu Plans to hand so you know exactly what you're going to be eating, and when.

● Make copies of the Daily Record Chart (see page 172), in which you will record each day of your weight loss journey

● Make copies of the Weekly Review (see page 173) – these are for identifying barriers to be bashed and implementing potential contingency plans when necessary.

Starting Line Form

Date: _ _ _ _ _ _ _ _ _ _

I have selected the _ _ _ _ _ _ _ _ _ _ Weight Loss Action Plan.

My current weight is: _ _ _ _ _ _ _ _ _ _

My goal weight is: _ _ _ _ _ _ _ _ _ _

My current measurements are: My goal measurements are:

Chest _ _ _ _ _ _ _ _ _ _   Chest _ _ _ _ _ _ _ _ _ _

Waist _ _ _ _ _ _ _ _ _ _   Waist _ _ _ _ _ _ _ _ _ _

Navel _ _ _ _ _ _ _ _ _ _   Navel _ _ _ _ _ _ _ _ _ _

Hips _ _ _ _ _ _ _ _ _ _   Hips _ _ _ _ _ _ _ _ _ _

Thigh _ _ _ _ _ _ _ _ _ _   Thigh _ _ _ _ _ _ _ _ _ _

I am starting my Action Plan on _ _ _ _ _ _ _ _ _ _

My estimated finish date is _ _ _ _ _ _ _ _ _ _

I am prepared to allow 10 per cent change to my end objectives.

My current energy needs are _ _ _ _ _ _ _ _ _ _

My current level of physical activity is _ _ _ _ _ _ _ _ _ _

I am going to try and achieve a daily 500 / 750 / 1000 calorie
Energy Gap (circle your choice)

New Phase Record Charts

Phase: _ _ _ _ _ _ _ _ _ _

My current weight is: _ _ _ _ _ _ _ _ _ _

My measurements are:

Chest _ _ _ _ _ _ _ _ _ _

Waist _ _ _ _ _ _ _ _ _ _

Navel _ _ _ _ _ _ _ _ _ _

Hips _ _ _ _ _ _ _ _ _ _

Thigh _ _ _ _ _ _ _ _ _ _

Waist circumference _ _ _ _ _ _ _ _ _ _

My percentage body fat is: _ _ _ _ _ _ _ _ _ _

My objective for this phase is: _ _ _ _ _ _ _ _ _ _

I feel (circle your choice):

Happy

Positive

Nervous

Confident

Use this daily checklist

● Simply remember to fill it in when you eat, and not at the end of the day – you will end up forgetting!

● Be sure to include all foods and drink you've had.

● Estimate portion sizes to the best of your ability (see page 117 if your memory needs refreshing).

● Include food preparation information whenever possible. (grilled, fried, roasted, baked, steamed, etc.).

Daily Record Chart

DAY: DATE:

BREAKFAST

LUNCH

DINNER (Remember to operate Carb Curfew)

Snack 1

Snack 2

Eating checklist:

Have I achieved Carb Curfew? YES / NO

Have I drunk 2 litres of water? YES / NO

Have I watched my fat intake? YES / NO

Have I had five portions of fruit and vegetables? YES / NO

Exercise checklist:

How many steps on my pedometer have I accumulated today?

_ _ _ _ _ _ _ _ _ _

Have I completed a Structured Exercise session today?
YES / NO

Weekly Review

This week I completed my Structured Exercise on the following days:

Monday ☐, Tuesday ☐, Wednesday ☐
Thursday ☐, Friday ☐, Saturday ☐, Sunday ☐

This week my daily accumulated step target on my pedometer was: _ _ _ _ _ _ _ _ _ or

This week my daily accumulated physical activity was _ _ _ _ _ _ _ _ _ minutes.

This week my daily calorie intake range was _ _ _ _ _ _ _ _ _

This week the barriers I bashed down were:

1. _
2. _
3. _

The barriers that I still need to bash down are:

1. _
2. _
3. _

My Contingency Plan is : _ _ _ _ _ _ _ _ _ _ _ _ _ _ _ _ _ _
_ _
_ _

I am going to put this in action on _ _ _ _ _ _ _ _ _

On reflection I feel I have had a:
Progressive week ☐
Maintenance week ☐
Damage limitation week ☐

My current weight is _ _ _ _ _ _ _ _ _
My goal weight is _ _ _ _ _ _ _ _ _

My current measurements are: My goal measurements are:
Chest _ _ _ _ _ _ _ _ _   Chest _ _ _ _ _ _ _ _ _
Waist _ _ _ _ _ _ _ _ _   Waist _ _ _ _ _ _ _ _ _
Navel _ _ _ _ _ _ _ _   Navel _ _ _ _ _ _ _ _
Hips _ _ _ _ _ _ _ _   Hips _ _ _ _ _ _ _ _ _
Thigh _ _ _ _ _ _ _ _   Thigh _ _ _ _ _ _ _ _

I am starting my Action Plan on _ _ _ _ _ _ _ _ _
My estimated finish date is _ _ _ _ _ _ _ _ _
I am prepared to allow 10 per cent change to my end objectives.

My current energy needs are _ _ _ _ _ _ _ _ _
My current level of physical activity is _ _ _ _ _ _ _ _ _

I am going to try and achieve a daily 500 / 750 / 1000 calorie Energy Gap (circle your choice)

Be consistent At this stage in your journey, it's time for me to remind you of a few crucial things:
- It's not how low you can take your calorie count, or how many excessive calories you can sweat off, but actually how consistent you can be with your efforts to create an Energy Gap that counts. Appreciating the importance of this right from the beginning can be a fundamental part of getting your body to work with you to lose weight and be on your winning side.
- Make sure you've put that One Night Stand approach we looked at in Chapter 1 a long way behind you now. After all, we've come a long way. Remember: this is about developing a long-term relationship with your body and nurturing your Template of Success.

Action Plan One

This plan is for those who want to lose around 20kg (44lb) — a weight loss equivalent to 20 standard bags of sugar. The plan takes 28 weeks to complete and has 7 phases, each lasting 4 weeks.

1 Weeks 1 to 4

Physical activity goals: Commit to 4 x 30-minute structured exercise sessions and a daily target of 7,000 steps, every day, by the time you complete this phase.

Healthy eating goals: Commit to implementing a Carb Curfew on at least 5 evenings each week.

2 Weeks 5 to 8

Physical activity goals: Commit to 4 Structured Exercise sessions (2 x 30 minutes, 2 x 45 minutes) and build up your daily steps target to 9,000 steps, every day, by the time you complete this phase.

Healthy eating goals: Implement the Carb Curfew every evening in this phase, and watch out for Portion Distortion. Aim to have your portions under control by the end of this phase, and to meet your calorie target.

3 Weeks 9 to 12

Physical activity goals: Commit to 4 x 45-minute Structured Exercise sessions and 10,000 steps a day, every day, by the time you complete this phase.

Healthy eating goals: Ensure calories do not dip below 1,500 a day, maintain the Carb Curfew and be sure to drink the required 2 litres of water a day.

Weeks 13 to 16

Physical activity goals: Consolidate your 10,000 accumulated daily steps achievement. Aim to make this your foundation by the end of this phase. Seek out contingency routes near your home and work, so you can easily incorporate these targets. Continue with your 4 structured exercise sessions each week.

Healthy eating goals: Make sure you are following the healthy eating advice in Chapter 5 and maintain your Carb Curfew. Eat 5 portions of fruit and vegetables, drink 2 litres of water, keep your fat intake below 60g (2oz) each day, and eat a portion of lean protein at each meal. Plan easy-to-prepare back-up meals as part of your contingency plans.

Weeks 17 to 20

Physical activity goals: Commit to 4 x 45–60-minute Structured Exercise sessions a week. To raise your energy expenditure in each session, introduce intervals of higher intensity in 2 out of 4 of your weekly sessions. Continue your 10,000 steps a day but on non-exercise days, try to raise your daily step total to 12,000, incorporating short bouts of break-point walking pace.

Healthy eating goals: Introduce soups in this phase as a way of volumising your food intake while cutting calories (see pages 154–5). Remember to plan your meals for each week ahead, perhaps on a Sunday, so you are better prepared for shopping.

Weeks 21 to 24

Physical activity goals: Commit to 4 x 45-minute structured exercise sessions and 10,000 steps a day. Introduce a relaxation class as one of your sessions in Week 2 and Week 4 of this phase. Try something new, such as Astanga yoga or Pilates.

Healthy eating goals: Give yourself one guilt-free night a week in this phase – try some of your less healthy favourites, but watch your portion sizes. Feel confident in your newfound skills and abilities.

Weeks 25 to 28

Physical activity goals: Commit to 4 x 60-minute structured exercise sessions, using interval-training techniques on 2 out of 4 of your weekly sessions. If you have the motivation and the time, add in one extra cardio session a week, and ideally make it a longer session – try a jog, or walk a route with your family or friends that takes at least 60 minutes. Ensure you complete your daily 10,000 steps as a minimum.

Healthy eating goals: Implement a double Carb Curfew in Week 25 and Week 27. Choose either lunch or breakfast as your other carb-free meal. One meal a day should have carbs.

Your Consistency Plan: now keep it off!

Physical activity goals: Commit to keeping up your 10,000 steps a day, along with brisk break-point walking and 4 structured exercise sessions each week.

Healthy eating goals: Keep within a calorie range of 1,500–1,800 for women, 1,600–2,000 for men, making sure you stick to all the healthy eating advice in Chapter 5.

Action Plan Two

This plan is for those who want to lose around 15kg (33lb) – a weight loss equivalent to 15 standard bags of sugar. The plan takes 20 weeks to complete and has 5 phases, each lasting 4 weeks.

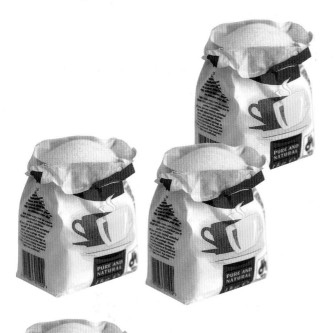

 **Weeks 1 to 4**

Physical activity goals: Commit to 4 x 30-minute structured exercise sessions and a daily target of 8,000 steps, every day, by the time you complete this phase.

Healthy eating goals: Commit to implementing a Carb Curfew at least 5 evenings each week.

Weeks 5 to 8

Physical activity goals: Commit to 4 structured exercise sessions (3 x 30 minutes, 1 x 45 minutes) and build up your step targets to 10,000 steps a day, every day, by the time you complete this phase.

Healthy eating goals: Implement a Carb Curfew every evening in this phase, and watch out for Portion Distortion. Aim to have your portions under control by the end of this phase and to meet your calorie target.

Weeks 9 to 12

Physical activity goals: Consolidate your 10,000 accumulated daily steps achievement. Aim to make this your foundation by the end of this phase. Seek out contingency routes near your home and work, so you can easily incorporate these targets. In addition complete your 4 x 45-minute structured exercise sessions each week.

Healthy eating goals: Check your nutrition intake and maintain your Carb Curfew. Eat 5 portions of fruit and vegetables, drink 2 litres of water, keep fat intake below 60g (2oz) each day, and eat a portion of lean protein at each meal. Plan back-up meals as contingency plans.

4 Weeks 13 to 16

Physical activity goals: Commit to 4 x 45–60-minute structured exercise sessions. To raise your energy expenditure in each session, introduce intervals of higher intensity in 1 out of 4 of your weekly sessions. Continue your 10,000 steps a day. On non-exercise days try to raise your step total to 12,000, incorporating short bouts of break-point walking.

Healthy eating goals: Introduce soups in this phase as a way of volumising your food intake while cutting calories (see pages 154–5). Remember to try to plan your meals for each week ahead, perhaps on a Sunday evening, so you are organised with your shopping and better prepared.

5 Weeks 17 to 20

Physical activity goals: Commit to 4 x 60-minute structured exercise sessions, using interval training techniques on 2 out of 4 of your weekly sessions. If you have the motivation and the time, add in one extra cardio session a week in this phase, and ideally make it a longer session – try a jog, or walk a route with your family or friend that takes at least 60 minutes. Ensure you complete your daily 10,000 steps as a minimum.

Healthy eating goals: Apply a double Carb Curfew in Week 17 and Week 19. You can choose either lunch or breakfast as your other carb-free meal but one meal a day should still contain some carbs.

Your Consistency Plan: now keep it off!

Physical activity goals: Commit to keep up your 10,000 steps a day, along with brisk break-point walking and 4 structured exercise sessions each week.

Healthy eating goals: Keep within a calorie range of 1,500–1,800 for women, 1,600–2,000 for men, making sure you stick to the healthy eating advice in Chapter 5.

Action Plan Three

This plan is for those who want to lose around 10kg (22lb) – a weight loss equivalent to 10 standard bags of sugar. The plan takes 12 weeks to complete and has 3 phases, each lasting 4 weeks.

1 Weeks 1 to 4

Physical activity goals: Commit to 4 x 40-minute structured exercise sessions a week and a target of 9,000 steps a day, every day, by the time you complete this phase.

Healthy eating goals: Commit to implementing a Carb Curfew at least 5 evenings each week in this phase, and try to stop Portion Distortion completely. By Week 3, introduce a mid-afternoon snack to keep your energy levels up.

2 Weeks 5 to 8

Physical activity goals: Commit to 4 structured exercise sessions (3 x 40 minutes, 1 x 50 minutes) and build up your steps target to 10,000 steps, every day, by the time you complete this phase. Try to introduce interval-style cardio work into your longer exercise session each week.

Healthy eating goals: Implement a Carb Curfew on all evening meals in this phase, and watch out for Portion Distortion. Aim to have your portion sizes under control by the end of this phase. By end of Week 7, ensure you are following all the healthy eating advice in Chapter 5. Give yourself one guilt-free night in Week 6 and Week 8 in this phase – if you feel like it, try some of your less healthy favourites, but with sensible portion control.

3 Weeks 9 to 12

Physical activity goals: Commit to 4 x 60-minute structured exercise sessions, using interval-training techniques during 2 out of 4 of your weekly sessions. If you have the motivation and the time, add in one extra cardio session a week, and ideally make it a longer session – try a jog, or walk a route with your family or a friend that takes at least 60 minutes to complete. Ensure you complete your daily 10,000 steps as a basic minimum level of activity.

Healthy eating goals: Implement a double Carb Curfew on 5 out of 7 days in weeks 9 and 11 of this phase. You can choose either lunch or breakfast as your other carb-free meal. One meal a day should still contain carbs. If you're hungry, go for vegetable soups.

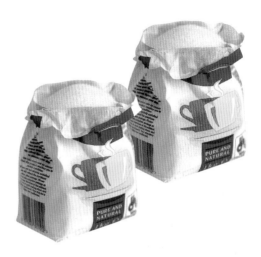

Your Consistency Plan: now keep it off!

Physical activity goals: Commit to 10,000 steps a day, along with brisk break-point walking for at least 5 minutes and 4 structured exercise cardio sessions each week.

Healthy eating goals: Keep within a calorie range of 1,500–1,800 for women, 1,600–2,000 for men, making sure you stick to the healthy eating advice in Chapter 5. Watch for Portion Distortion.

The 80:20 Rule: Being consistent means you need to be good on average 80 per cent of the time. This allows about a 20 per cent margin for mismanagement, or slipping off the wagon. You'll still manage to lose weight and keep it off. In my experience this rule has been enormously reassuring for my clients once they have dropped their weight.

Action Plan Four

There are two plans for those who want to lose around 5kg (11lb) – a weight loss equivalent to 5 bags of sugar. The Fast Track plan is more rigid, for when you want results quickly. It takes 5 weeks and is split into 2 phases. The more gently paced plan takes 7 weeks and also has 2 phases.

Fast Track

1 Weeks 1 to 3

Physical activity goals: Commit to 4 x 45-minute structured exercise sessions each week, and a target of 10,000 steps a day, every day, by the time you complete this phase. Try to hit 8,000 steps every day by end of Week 2.

Healthy eating goals: Commit to implementing a Carb Curfew at least 5 evenings each week, and try to stop Portion Distortion completely. By Week 3 make sure you are eating a mid-afternoon snack, since it will keep your energy levels up.

2 Weeks 4 to 5

Physical activity goals: Commit to 4 x 60-minute structured exercise sessions, using interval-training techniques in 2 out of 4 of your weekly sessions. If you have the motivation and the time, add in one extra cardio session a week in this phase, and ideally make it a longer session – try a jog, or walk a route with your family or friend that takes at least 60 minutes. Ensure you complete your daily 10,000 steps as a minimum. Revisit break-point walking, as this will ensure you are optimising your walking time and getting fitter and healthier at the same time.

Healthy eating goals: Implement a double Carb Curfew on 3 out of 7 days in Week 4 and in Week 5 enforce it on 4 out of 7 days. You can choose either lunch or breakfast as your other carb-free meal. One meal a day should contain carbs. If you're hungry, go for vegetable soups. You should feel happy with portion control and aim to have your energy-boosting breakfasts working well.

Your Consistency Plan: now keep it off!

Physical activity goals: Commit to 10,000 steps a day, along with brisk break-point walking for at least 5 minutes each day. Add in 4 structured exercise cardio sessions each week.

Healthy eating goals: Keep within a calorie range of 1,500–1,800 for women, 1,600–2,000 for men, making sure you stick to the healthy eating advice in Chapter 5. Watch for Portion Distortion.

Gentle Track

1 Weeks 1 to 4

Physical activity goals: Commit to 4 x 40-minute structured exercise sessions each week, and a daily target of 9,000 steps a day, every day, by the time you complete this phase. Try to hit 8,000 steps every day by the end of Week 3.

Healthy eating goals: Commit to implementing a Carb Curfew at least 6 evenings each week. Try to stop Portion Distortion completely. By Week 3 you should be implementing Carb Curfew every night. Make sure you are eating a mid-afternoon snack, since it will keep your energy levels up.

2 Weeks 5 to 7

Physical activity goals: Commit to 4 x 60-minute structured exercise sessions, using interval-training techniques on 2 out of 4 of your weekly sessions. If you have the motivation and the time, add in one extra cardio session a week. If you can't introduce it right from the start, make sure you fit in at least 2 extra sessions by the end of this phase, and ideally make it a longer session – try a jog, or walk a route with your family or a friend that takes at least 60 minutes. Ensure you complete your daily 10,000 steps as a minimum. Revisit break-point walking, as this will ensure you are optimising your walking time while getting fitter and healthier. Introduce the Waistband Whittler workout in 3 out of 4 of your structured workouts.

Healthy eating goals: Implement a double Carb Curfew on 3 out of 7 days in weeks 5 and 6, and in Week 7 enforce it on 4 out of 7 days. You can choose either lunch or breakfast as your other carb-free meal. One meal a day should contain carbs. If you're still hungry, go for vegetable soups. You should feel happy with portion control and aim to have your energy-boosting breakfasts in hand.

Your Consistency Plan: now keep it off!

Physical activity goals: Commit to 10,000 steps a day, along with brisk break-point walking for at least 5 minutes each day, and add in 4 structured exercise cardio sessions in each week. Complete the Waistband Whittler workout on 4 out of 7 days a week.

Healthy eating goals: Keep within a calorie range of 1,500–1,800 for women, 1,600–2,000 for men, making sure you stick to the healthy eating advice in Chapter 5. Watch out for Portion Distortion. Implement a double Carb Curfew twice a week .

Action Plan Five

There are two plans for those who want to lose around 2kg (4.5lb) — a weight loss equivalent to 2 bags of sugar. The Fast Track plan is more rigid, for when you want results quickly. It takes 2 weeks and is split into 2 phases. The more gently paced plan takes 4 weeks and also has 2 phases. You don't have much weight to lose, but you will have to stick to the Action Plan you choose fairly strictly to make a difference in such a short time.

Your Consistency Plan: now keep it off!

Physical activity goals: You need to make sure that your daily 10,000 step achievement is the foundation of your new lifestyle if you want to keep the weight off. Revisit break-point walking at least twice a week to optimise your walking. Keep up the 4 structured exercise sessions each week. Ideally, if you're short of time, aim to make at least 2 sessions interval-style, the third session your longest workout session, and your fourth based on toning and stretching (such as Pilates or Astanga yoga).

Healthy eating goals: Gradually increase your calorie intake to the level you need (see page 116). Keep your portions under control and maintain your 2-litre a day water intake. Practise a double Carb Curfew twice a week to keep you on track.

Fast Track

Week 1

Physical activity goals: Build up to 10,000 steps a day, along with brisk break-point walking for at least 10 minutes each day, broken into 2 bouts of 5 minutes. Add in 4 structured exercise cardio sessions each week, making one of them a more gentle toning-style workout from the appropriate Body Shape workouts (see pages 88–99). Include the Waist Whittler workout (see pages 80–6) in at least 3 sessions.

Healthy eating goals: Keep within a calorie range of 1,500–1,800 for women, 1,600–2,000 for men, making sure you stick to the healthy eating advice in Chapter 5. Watch out for Portion Distortion, and implement a double Carb Curfew on 4 of the 7 days this week. Make sure you have a good breakfast every day, front-loading your day to stop it becoming bottom-heavy with calories.

Week 2

Physical activity goals: Consolidate your 10,000 steps, along with brisk break-point walking for at least 10 minutes each day, broken into 2 bouts of 5 minutes, one in the morning and one later in the day. Add in 4 structured exercise cardio sessions each week, select your Body Shape workout and commit to this 3 times this week as part of your structured exercise session. If you've time, add in a fifth session, making one of them a more gentle, toning-style workout (such as Pilates or Astanga yoga). Make sure you include the Waist Whittler workout on at least 3 of these sessions.

Healthy eating goals: Keep within a calorie range of 1,500–1,800 for women, 1,600–2,000 for men, making sure you stick to the healthy eating advice in Chapter 5. Watch out for Portion Distortion, and commit to a double Carb Curfew on 4 of the 7 days this week. Make sure you front-load your day by having a good breakfast.

Gentle Track

1 Weeks 1 and 2

Physical activity goals: Build up to 10,000 steps a day, along with brisk break-point walking for at least 5 minutes each day, broken into 2 bouts of 5 minutes by end of Week 1. Raise this to 10 minutes by the end of Week 2. Add 4 structured exercise cardio sessions in each week, making one of them a more gentle, toning-style workout designed for your body shape. Make sure you include the Waist Whittler workout in at least 3 of these sessions each week.

Healthy eating goals: Keep within a calorie range of 1,500–1,800 for women, 1,600–2,000 for men, making sure you stick to the healthy eating advice in Chapter 5. Watch out for Portion Distortion, and commit to a double Carb Curfew on 3 of the 7 days this week. Make sure you have a good breakfast every day, front-loading your day to avoid becoming bottom-heavy with calories.

2 Weeks 3 and 4

Physical activity goals: Consolidate your daily 10,000 steps with brisk break-point walking for at least 10 minutes each day, broken into 2 bouts of 5 minutes, one in the morning and one later in the day. Add in 4 structured exercise cardio sessions each week, select your Body Shape workout and commit to this three times in Week 3, and 4 times in Week 4, as part of your structured exercise session. If you've time, add a fifth session, making this one a more gentle, toning-style workout (such as Pilates or Astanga yoga). Make sure you include the Waist Whittler workout at least 4 days of each week.

Healthy Eating Goals: Keep within a calorie range of 1,500–1,800 for women, 1,600–2,000 for men, making sure you stick to the healthy eating advice in Chapter 5. Watch out for Portion Distortion, and commit to a double Carb Curfew on 4 of the 7 days in Week 3, and on 5 of the 7 days in Week 4. Make sure you have a good breakfast every day, front-loading to avoid becoming bottom-heavy with calories.

Your Consistency Plan: now keep it off!

Physical activity goals: You need to make sure the 10,000 daily steps achievement is the foundation of your new lifestyle. Revisit break-point walking at least twice a week to optimise your walking. Keep up the 4 structured exercise sessions each week. Ideally, if you're short of time, aim to make at least two sessions interval-style, the third session your longest workout, and your fourth session mostly toning and stretching (such as Pilates or Astanga yoga).

Healthy eating goals: Gradually raise your calorie intake to the level you need (see page 116). Keep your portions under control, follow the healthy eating advice and ensure you're drinking your daily 2 litres of water. Practise a double Carb Curfew twice a week to keep you on track.

Barrier Bashing

I'm sure you remember that barrier bashing involves identifying what you think may pose a challenge to your efforts, and then a little problem-solving and planning ahead to devise ways of bashing it down, so that you can continue on your journey. Once you've developed strategies to keep up your sleeve, you can always prevent or at least minimise a potential challenge.

Below is a list of some of the barriers I have come across with my clients, along with solutions we devised, and I hope that you will find them useful too. Of course, you'll have some barriers that are unique to you, and you'll have to invent strategies for bashing them down yourself.

Barrier: Arrive home starving!

This is one of the most common times when people get into trouble with those addictive foods.

Bash it down: Have a snack after work, because this will take the edge off your hunger and may help stop you over-eating at dinner too. Make sure you have a ready supply of fruits, nuts, or other non-trigger foods in the house that you put aside especially for this time. Alternatively, stop off at a coffee shop on the way home and instead of ordering a large coffee, have a large cup of skimmed milk to curb your hunger.

At social events:

Alcohol, soft drinks, cheesy snacks, bread, sweets and other common trigger foods are likely to be offered. Before you head out, eat a handful of nuts, a piece of fruit or another non-trigger food, or make yourself a smoothie before you go. Look at the Menu Plans for snack ideas.

Party Time!

Parties can present a tricky barrier on your weight loss journey – but they don't have to be your downfall. With a little navigation and pre-planning, you *can* go to the ball!

Alternative snacks

Instead of...	*Choose...*
2 sausage rolls (480 calories)	3 cocktail sausages (260 calories)
30g slice of quiche (141 calories)	a 90g chicken drumstick (130 calories)
28g of salami (120 calories)	28g turkey breast (35 calories)
4 glasses of red wine (380 calories)	4 white wine spritzers (200 calories)
Scooping your dips with crackers, breadsticks, pitta bread and tortilla chips (365 calories)	Scoop your dips with crudités (1 calorie per vegetable stick)
a packet of crisps (150 calories)	a pack of Twiglets (95 calories)
4 After Eights (140 calories)	4 satsumas (100 calories)
6 chocolate brazil nuts (330 calories)	6 dates (90 calories)

The lowdown on liquid calories

Drink	*Liquid calories*
1 x 275ml bottle low-alcohol lager	40
1 medium sherry	60
1 port	70
1 x 175ml glass of orange juice	70
1 x 275ml bottle Pils	75
1 gin and diet tonic	85
1 x 125ml glass dry white/red wine	85
1 x 125ml glass of champagne	95
1 half pint lager	100
1 Pimms and lemonade	110
1 x 125ml glass sweet white wine	118
1 rum and coke	123
1 x 330 ml glass Pina Colada	486

Liquid calories can easily add up, but with some wise choices you can still enjoy a drink or two without it cutting into your Energy Gap too much. Space out your alcoholic drinks by having a large glass of water in between.

Four great party tricks

● Eat before you go out. Plan your snacks so you don't arrive at the party starving – it will be your biggest downfall. Remember to keep well hydrated right through the day of your party, too, as this can help minimise hunger and the effects of a heavy night.

● Know your dips. Go for salsa ones (5 calories per 10g scoop) or tsatziki (10 calories per 10g scoop). They're lower in calories (and fat) than creamy dips, such as sour cream or taramasalata.

● Try 'spicy' drinks. A tomato juice with a dash of Tabasco sauce won't stimulate your appetite nearly as much as sweeter drinks (whether they're alcoholic or not).

● Don't stand anywhere near the bowls of crisps and nuts or you'll end up grazing all evening.

Festive fare at home

● Eat your mince pies topless! If you have a mince pie fetish at Christmas time, go for the ones without the pastry lid: they only have 160 calories, while ordinary mince pies weigh in at over 200 calories. And, if you usually eat them with cream (170 calories per 45g), try low-fat fromage frais (35 calories per 30g) instead.

● Eat your Christmas cake naked! An average slice will set you back about 418 calories. Take off the icing and marzipan, however, and you'll save yourself about 239 calories.

Barrier: Stress makes me crave carbs!

Carbs trigger the production of a feel-good hormone called serotonin, which helps to boost your mood and temporarily relieve your stress.

Bash it down: Give in to a carb-rich lunch occasionally. Using food for temporary relief from a problem is fine as long as you don't do it all the time. Plan your menus in a way that allows you to enjoy chicken nuggets with potato wedges every now and then. Better still, try to eat a very small portion of carbs along with a high-protein food such as steak, chicken or tuna salad. Stride out stress as well – when really stressed, go out for a brisk, 15-minute, stress-busting walk.

Barrier: The 4 o'clock chocolate hour

Your energy levels are low and you are slumping big-time – chocolate seems the only answer!

Bash it down: Give in – but just a little. If you have an intense craving for a very specific food – like chocolate (and remember, chocolate contains an addictive, mood-altering substance) – I think it's best to go ahead and eat it. If you don't, your craving is going to get more intense until you eventually give in anyway and you will have consumed a lot of unnecessary calories in your attempt to make it go away. Have a glass of milk and 2 cubes of dark chocolate, as I've set out on the menu plans. Pre-planning these will help you feel more in control.

If you do succumb to biscuits, make sure you keep the lapse under control – meaning take two or three biscuits or pieces of chocolate at most, and then put the rest away. You may feel as if you want more, but it's worth knowing that according to a study conducted at Pennsylvania State University people who

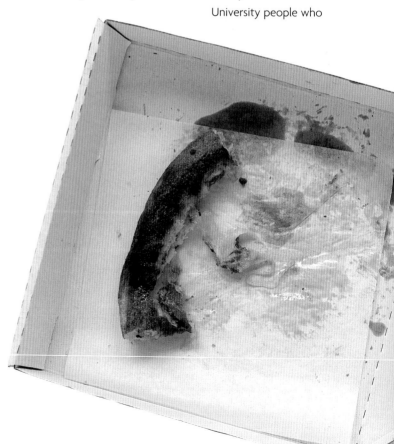

were served the smallest portions of a food felt just as full and satisfied as those who were given unlimited helpings of the same food.

If you do lapse big-time, then make a note of it on your weekly review and choose an appropriate action from your contingency plan.

Barrier: Evening crisp craving

In the evening you want to relax. The crisp craving that strikes at this time is less about the food and more about what the food signifies – chilling out and maybe rewarding yourself after a tough day.

Bash it down: Fight the urge to eat – you are eating for the wrong reason. When it happens too often, this kind of emotionally driven eating becomes a primary reason for weight gain. To break the habit, bite the bullet and go cold turkey – no food while the TV's on.

Create food-free zones, such as 6.30–8pm, since even healthy snacks won't help break the association between food and relaxing. To make the process easier, decide to do something during that time that doesn't involve sitting down, such as rearranging the living-room furniture. Studies suggest

that hanging out in the same spot where you have indulged past cravings can trigger new ones.

Barrier: Pre-bed ice-cream urge

This is a fairly natural urge, since carbohydrates help to boost levels of a sleep-inducing compound called tryptophan. As tryptophan levels in your brain increase, you become sleepier.

Bash it down: Say no! Opt for a glass of warm milk or a low-calorie hot chocolate drink. Alternatively, say yes! No, you're not misreading this; if saying no just doesn't work, go ahead and give in to the ice-cream. Better that than hunger keeping you awake. Keep the serving small and pick a regular, full-fat ice-cream – not the fat-free kind, because you may well end up eating more of it. According to a study from Purdue, taste buds can detect fat and that may be why fat-free foods aren't as satisfying as full-fat foods.

Barrier: I'm still hungry after dinner!

This may be because you are eating too quickly rather than not eating enough. It takes 20 minutes for the stretch receptors in your stomach lining to send a message to the brain registering food – by that time, you may have eaten well beyond your calorie needs. Eating too quickly can cause digestive problems and is thought to be a cause of irritable bowel syndrome.

Bash it down: Time how long it takes you to eat each meal. Then try to give yourself longer to finish each one, starting off by aiming to increase your recorded time by 50 per cent for one whole week. The following week, try to add a further 50 per cent. Eat until you are 80 per cent full. You know what 100 per cent full feels like, so stop short before you get to that point. At first, this may feel an alien thing to do but persevere with this – it allows your brain to become aware of how food feels as it starts to enter your body, stopping you from over-eating and actually energising you more. Eating too much food decreases your immediate energy levels, as your body has to work harder to digest your food. Stopping short of finishing should also empower you, as you'll feel more in control of your food volume.

Barrier: I'm going out to dinner

You must have realised by now that I firmly believe living a healthy, balanced life includes going out and having a good time. You don't have to put your weight loss journey on hold just because some friends invite you for an evening out.

Bash it down: Instead of sticking to your Carb Curfew dinner and causing all sorts of complications for your host, have a starch curfew lunch instead. This allows you to include some starch with your evening meal without over-indulging.

This one's a useful strategy for those of us who over-eat when away from our home territory. Divide the food on your plate in two halves. If you are dining out, you can make an imaginary line. Eat half the food. Stop for 10 minutes and either leave the table, or sip a glass of water until it's empty. If you are still hungry after 10 minutes, finish your meal. If you are not sure, divide the remainder in half and repeat the exercise in exactly the same way.

Order first, drink later. Alcohol loosens your inhibitions, making you less careful when ordering. It also leaves you feeling less satisfied after your meal, resulting in an increased calorie intake over the next 24 hours.

My usual, please! If you're going to a restaurant that you know, decide beforehand what you would like to order, basing your choice on your Action Plan. That way, you won't be tempted by high-calorie specials when you open the menu. There are tips on dishes to opt for in different kinds of restaurant on pages 190–1.

BODY LAID BARE...

How to survive eating out

If you're afraid to eat out in case your good intentions and resolve weaken when you're confronted with an exciting restaurant menu, don't be. All you have to do is try to stick to the low-fat, vitamin-rich menu choices outlined here. The golden rule is to avoid anything fried, as this will be overloaded with fat – and our fat cells love to feed on fatty foods. Remember, as well, to apply the Carb Curfew where possible – but if you really want some carbs, you can shift your Curfew to the middle of your day so that lunch becomes your Carb Free Zone! (And if all else fails, there are always the Contingency Plans at the end of this chapter!)

Read that menu carefully

British menus

- Ask for a prawn cocktail without the dressing.
- Minestrone and consommé are low-fat starters.
- If you're allowing yourself carbs, choose boiled or jacket potatoes instead of roast.
- Skip the gravy – choose mint sauce, mustard or herb seasonings instead.
- Don't eat the skin on roast chicken or duck.
- Request plain vegetables without butter.
- Avoid cooked breakfasts; cereal is a lower-fat option.

American menus

- Choose a restaurant with a self-service salad bar.
- Avoid pre-dressed salads and instead dress your own with seasoned vinegars, or lemon juice and herbs.
- Use mayonnaise, ketchup and relishes sparingly.
- Choose baked potatoes instead of chips and don't add butter or sour cream.

Indian menus

- Curries can be very high in fat; choose vegetable options and avoid dishes like chicken korma, which contain cream.
- Indian flat breads are a good choice and better than poppadoms, which are deep-fried.
- Basmati rice is an excellent option.
- Avoid deep-fried onion and vegetable bhajis.

Chinese menus

● Fried rice is very high in fat; choose boiled rice which has almost no fat at all.

● Request boiled noodles instead of fried noodles.

● Tofu (bean curd) is a low-fat protein option that is found in many oriental dishes.

● Stir-fried vegetables are a good choice.

● Don't be tempted to snack on prawn crackers – they are deep-fried so have a high-fat content.

● Avoid spring rolls – these also contain a great deal of fat.

● Cashew nuts are high in saturated fat.

● Beansprouts and water chestnuts are a good option.

● Lychees are an excellent, low-fat choice for dessert.

Italian menus

● Minestrone soup, melon and trimmed Parma ham are low-fat starters.

● Skinless breast of chicken and grilled fish dishes are a good choice.

● Choose a simple tomato sauce for pasta and only add a small sprinkling of Parmesan cheese.

● Avoid high-fat carbonara, cream or cheese sauces.

● Chargrilled vegetables or seafood are a tasty, low fat option – but watch for the excessive use of olive oil, which can often be deceptive.

● Choose sorbet or fresh fruit instead of ice-cream for dessert.

● Cappuccino coffee can add extra unnecessary calories; opt for mint or camomile tea instead; alternatively, if caffeine is a necessity an espresso is a better choice.

Japanese menus

● Miso soup with noodles and vegetables is a good choice.

● Sasami and seaweed salad is an excellent choice, rich in protein, essential fats and iodine.

● Soba noodles, made with buckwheat, are low in fat.

● Nori rolls (rice wrapped in seaweed) are deliciously low calorie.

● Boiled rice is better than high-fat fried rice.

● Chicken or beef teriyaki and raw fish sushi or sashimi are also good, low-fat choices.

Middle Eastern menus

● Taboulleh salad made with cracked wheat and herbs is good choice.

● Houmous (made without cream) and yoghurt dips served with pitta breads are healthy options.

● Try to avoid taramasalata, as this can be a hidden calorie holder.

● Vine leaves stuffed with raisin rice, couscous dishes and savoury lentils are all good choices.

● Avoid deep-fried falafel, *fatayer* and samosas.

● Opt for *baba ganoush* (puréed aubergines with lemon juice), kebabs served with salad, *shashlik* (marinated meat or veg on a skewer) or grilled meat and fish dishes.

Barrier: We don't have time for proper dinners

Not eating as a family can cultivate some bad eating habits for everyone – one survey showed that overweight children ate at least half of their meals in front of the television. Others revealed that youngsters who had dinner with their parents ate lower-fat foods, chose more fruit and vegetables, and were less prone to anxiety and depression, regardless of their social background.

Bash it down: Make a family dinner date. Mark everyone's calendars and tell them their attendance at dinner is requested. You could even write invitations to make it more of a special occasion.

If time's definitely your problem, bring home healthy fast food. Try pre-cut, frozen, canned or microwave-in-the-bag veg. Turn up the nutrition on canned soups by adding frozen vegetables and pre-cooked chicken breasts. Dig out the slow cooker. Toss in frozen chicken breasts, a bag of frozen carrots, chopped onions and a jar of low-salt sauce before you leave for work. Your meal will be ready when you get home.

Sit down on the run. If you only have time for a quick bite at a fast-food restaurant you can still make it a healthy affair. For example, choose grilled chicken with no sauce and remove the skin, or a single burger with lettuce and tomato instead of a triple cheeseburger. Order side salads (hold the dressing) and skip the fizzy drinks, opting instead for low-fat milk, water and juice. Unfortunately, pizza can be a minefield, laden with cheese, high-fat meat and oil. The main problem, however, is the size of the helping you're usually given. If you're eating out, share a pizza with a friend and fill up with a side salad. Or ask the restaurant to use half the usual amount of cheese, substituting it for a variety of vegetable toppings.

Barrier: Buffets

Buffets are the dieter's downfall. An American study recently found that people ate a staggering 44 per cent more when they were able to select from a variety of dishes.

Bash it down: Try limiting your variety of foods to two per plate; that way you are not over-eating all in one go. Allow

yourself to go back as many times as you wish, but enjoy the flavours you have on your plate one at one time.

Stop Portion Distortion. Fill your plate with vegetables, salad and lower-calorie foods and then top it off with one or two of the other buffet fillers, remembering to keep a check on portion sizes. Turn back to page 117 if you need reminding.

Prioritise your eating. Once back at your table, eat the lowest calorie foods first (these are generally the vegetables). Then eat the next lowest calorie item. Save your highest calorie item for last. You'll get the taste, but you may just find yourself too full to finish it.

Barrier: Weekends

When there's less of a routine, you let it all go.

Bash it down: Try the two-meal tool. At weekends, we often have two meals quite close together. Many of us have breakfast late and then lunch an hour or two later. Both these meals will also tend to be a bit bigger than you would have during the week. Save calories by having just two meals a day at weekends, breakfast (or brunch) and dinner, and just a snack in between.

Cook on a full stomach. If you have to bake or prepare for a dinner party, try to do it when you are full, after a meal or in the morning. You'll be less inclined to nibble.

Stretch your lunch. If you know you always get hungry in the afternoon, split your lunch into two sittings. Eat half at your normal lunchtime and the remaining half in the afternoon – but make sure you sit down for it rather than eating it at the fridge.

Barrier: Menstrual cycle

Many women find that try as they might, they just can't resist those food cravings before and/or during a period. This is quite natural – studies show that in the two weeks leading up to your period, your metabolic rate actually increases by about 140 calories. The problem is that the chocolate bar you are craving will, on average, provide 250 calories.

Bash it down: If you really feel you are not going to be able to resist a binge, allocate a binge zone of up to a couple of hours. This is a time when you allow yourself to binge, but eat your fill of the lowest-calorie foods possible – try bowls of water-packed fruits such as strawberries or melon, or some steamed veg. You will fill yourself up, but stay within your calorie limit.

If you still lapse, then take it on the chin and adopt a contingency plan the following day.

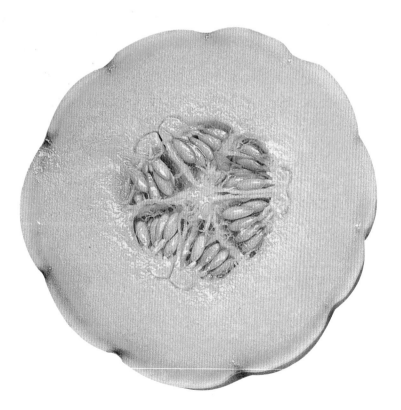

Instead of a 250-calorie chocolate bar, select one of the following 100 calorie snacks:

2 squares Dairy Milk chocolate

2 oatcakes

any piece of fruit

20 almonds

8 dried apricots

1 small pot low-fat yoghurt

a palmful of sunflower and pumpkin seeds

2 rice cakes topped with cottage cheese

half a small avocado filled with salsa

(You'll find more to choose from on page 121)

Barrier: I feel powerless to stop myself

If you are binge-eating regularly, you need to work on your Template of Success, and you might like to start by revisiting the steps to self-esteem on pages 18–19. Meantime, the following tips might help at the moment the urge strikes.

Bash it down: Take time out, and disconnect temporarily from everything food-related. Remember: you are in control, but you need to give yourself some space to realise this. Get up from the table, brush your teeth, or stop and clean a room in the house. Do whatever it takes to give yourself a break.

Switch the taste sensation. You can help stop a binge in its tracks by switching to a completely different food the moment you catch yourself at the point of bingeing. So, if you have started to polish off a carton of ice-cream, put the carton away and pull out a bag of fruit or carrot sticks. It will give you an opportunity to create some distance from the easy-eating, high-calorie food.

Barrier: I travel so much

Being away from your normal environment can be a killer. Your routine is shot to pieces, you mainly eat out, you may have to decipher different food cultures, and, of course, you're just plain tired.

Bash it down: Pre-order your aeroplane meal. Most airlines are quite happy to do this, but they tend not to make it public knowledge. There is a wide range of special meals you can order – low fat, low calorie, low cholesterol, kosher, vegetarian, to name a few. Watch out for the veggie option, as it is almost invariably high in fat. I'd recommend you request a low calorie rather than the low-fat meal as I have found the latter often turns out to be a low cholesterol meal that still has a high fat content. And remember to say no to the bread roll and drink plenty of water.

Plan some prior protein! Make sure your last pre-travel meal contains a good balance of protein and starch, so you feel satisfied and motivated. Athletes journeying to international competitions use this strategy to minimise the detrimental effects of travelling on their performance. Before a long drive, have less protein but with lots of vegetables and fruit. Remember not to eat too much or your blood sugar levels will rise too quickly and you'll feel lethargic.

Blinker out the sweets at the garage counter. If you must buy something, grab some chewing gum and a bottle of water.

Pack your pedometer. You may not feel like exercising as soon as you arrive at your destination but do try to move your body – resolve to get 4,000 steps on that pedometer as soon as possible. It's a great way to explore, and it'll help you get rid of travel fatigue. If you are on a business trip and your structured exercise sessions are just not going to happen, resolve to get in your daily 10,000 steps – even if it means getting up a little earlier.

Avoid excess baggage! If you are at a bar, or are offered nibbles with your pre-dinner drink, say NO – they are laden with salt and calories. Implement a Carb Curfew wherever possible. It works at home and it works just as well when you're away. Try varieties of fruit and vegetables that aren't available at home, and restrict starchy foods to lunchtimes.

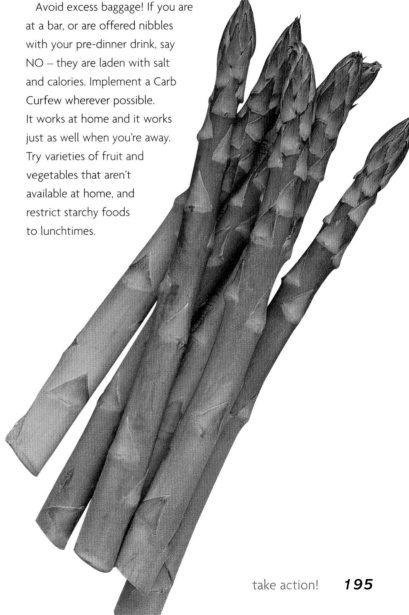

Contingency Plans

A contingency plan is an action that is put in place once you feel you have taken a back step on your weight loss journey, or perhaps a wrong turn. The aim of your contingency plan is to help you get back on track and keep on track, so that your lapse does not become a collapse. Contingency plans stop you feeling like you are failing – they put you firmly in control, reinforcing your Template of Success, and stopping a Template of Failure taking hold. Contingency plans involve some adjustment to your Energy Gap plans – either some sort of extra energy burn or short-term dietary adjustment.

1 Play the 300 calorie game

If you know you are heading for a weekend of excess, don't starve yourself all week. Instead eat 300 fewer calories the day before your partying begins and be sure to fit in a structured exercise session. Then eat 300 fewer calories the day after. I'd advise you to cut back on a snack or limit portions rather than missing out a whole meal, which may only serve to distort your energy levels even further, leaving you wanting more sugary, quick-fix comfort foods. If your body feels up to it, fit in another Structured Exercise session, but you may find it more appropriate to stick to your walking targets – especially if you have a sore head! Carry on being consistent through the rest of the week.

2 Double Carb Curfew

If you have a weekend of weddings, parties or other back-to-back social events, introduce a double Carb Curfew – lunch and supper – but do still have some slow-releasing carbs at breakfast. I suggest this because the chances are your fat intake will be higher on these days, pushing up your calorie intake, and it will be easier to avoid carbs than fatty foods. Try to follow all the party tips and tricks on pages 185–6 and you won't go too far off track.

3 Stay hydrated

After a weekend of excess you will feel tired – make sure you don't compound it by being dehydrated as well. Remember to drink little and often, so that you don't misinterpret your thirst for hunger.

4 Veg-up!

If you have really pigged out, your stomach may well have stretched and it will take more food to make you feel satisfied. Use liquid foods to help curb your hunger and preserve your Energy Gap. All you have to do is make yourself up a cauldron of vegetable soup (see recipe, right) to eat before you go out in the evening – this will curb your appetite and line your stomach.

5 Burn those calories

Sometimes you just have to accept that you will need to go out and burn a little more energy, whether it is through Active Travel, a Workout Wedge or longer Structured Exercise. Here are some quick and easy ways to expend roughly 100 calories:

- Walk a mile
- Accumulate 2,000 steps on your pedometer
- Complete 500 skips
- Walk up and down stairs for 5 minutes continuously
- Dance enthusiastically to your favourite music for 12 non-stop minutes.

Here's a great recipe for a hearty vegetable soup. If you don't fancy such a filling meal, consider the smoothie options on page 129 or the fresh juices on page 108.

Hearty Vegetable Soup

Serves 4

It's a good idea to make double and freeze for later.

2 teaspoons olive oil
1 onion, chopped
1/2 head cabbage, cut into 5cm pieces
2 carrots, cut into 2.5cm pieces
2 celery stalks, cut into 2.5cm pieces
1 courgette, cut into 2.5cm pieces
4 small red potatoes (with skin), cut into 2.5cm pieces
225g fresh mushrooms, sliced
6 tomatoes, peeled, seeded and diced
400ml chicken or vegetable stock
15g fresh chopped basil
1 tbsp fresh thyme, chopped
1/2 teaspoon salt
1/2 teaspoon freshly ground black pepper

1 Heat the oil in a large pan over a medium heat. Add the onion and cabbage and sauté until tender (about 5 minutes). Add the carrots, celery, courgette, potatoes and mushrooms and simmer for 5 minutes.

2 Add the tomatoes, stock, basil, thyme, salt and pepper. Bring to the boil, reduce the heat to low and simmer until the potatoes are tender (about 30 minutes).

Note: If you are on a Carb Curfew, you can omit the potatoes.

Maintaining your weight loss

Most of what we know about people who have lost weight and kept it off comes from university-based weight loss programmes, as few of the commercial programmes tend to collect or publish data.

The National Weight Control Registry is an American study founded in 1993 by professors at the University of Colorado and the University of Pittsburgh. Before they are signed up, dieters must have lost at least 14kg (30lb) each and have kept it off for minimum of a year. In fact the average weight loss is 27kg (60lb) per person and they have kept it off for an average of 5 years – they like to be known as 'Successful Losers'. This makes them an extremely valuable group to study when formulating successful weight-loss strategies.

They all had four strategies in common:

● Eating a low-fat, high-carbohydrate diet of 1,300 to 1,500 calories per day (of which only 23 per cent to 24 per cent came from fat).

● Eating breakfast almost every day.

● Frequently monitoring their weight – this serves as an 'early warning system'.

● Maintaining a high level of physical activity. The mean energy they expended was 2,000 kcal a week for women and 3,300 kcal a week for men, with walking being the most popular form of exercise. This equates to about 60 to 90 minutes of moderate-intensity physical activity per day.

If you want to maintain, you need to move!

Interestingly, 89 per cent of Registry participants used both diet and physical activity to lose weight; only 10 per cent used diet alone, and 1 per cent used exercise alone. This finding is very important because most weight loss programmes focus primarily on dietary restriction with little attention to effective physical activity. Only 9 per cent of Registry participants reported keeping their weight off without engaging in physical activity.

Walking appeared to be the most popular form of physical activity, but most people also engaged in some planned structured exercise. Twenty-eight per cent of participants used only walking as their chosen form of physical activity, and about half combined walking with another form of planned exercise, such as aerobics classes, cycling or swimming. A sample of the participants were given pedometers to quantify their walking, which revealed that, on average, they took between 11,000 and 12,000 steps (about 9–10km/5^{1}/$_{2}$–6 miles) per day.

If you want to follow in the footsteps of the Successful Losers, I hope you know by now what you have to do!

How to be a successful loser:

● Eat a low-fat, high-carbohydrate diet

● Eat breakfast almost every day

● Weigh yourself frequently

● Engage in 60 to 90 minutes per day of moderate-intensity physical activity (this is probably the most significant factor of all in keeping weight off).

7 your children's weight

Why are children gaining weight?

Children have always loved to jump, run and play; in fact, being active is the natural state of affairs for most kids. So how is it, then, that we are faced with a whole new generation of overweight children? Kids who choose the games console over playing in the park, watching TV over a bike ride with their friends, sitting slumped in front of a video rather than racing up and down the stairs? The food our children eat is obviously a major factor in their weight gain, but so too is this increased inactivity. The Energy Gap is just as relevant for kids — if they are inactive and eating the wrong foods, their weight will rise. And rise it has!

According to the International Obesity Task Force, some 22 million of the world's under-fives are now overweight or obese. In the UK, the government estimates that the number of overweight children has increased by 25 per cent since 1995, with almost 17 per cent of UK children now classified as obese. Obesity among six-year-olds has doubled in recent years to 8.5 per cent and trebled to 15 per cent among 15-year-olds — and note, these figures are for 'obese' children; not those who are simply overweight. Some leading medical experts warn that more than one in three adults, one in five boys and one in three girls will be obese by 2020 if current trends continue.

Won't they outgrow it?

The popular notion that most overweight children will 'lose their puppy fat' as they grow up is false. Baylor Medical School in the US reports that approximately 40 per cent of obese seven-year-olds and 70 per cent of obese adolescents become obese adults. The older your child gets, the harder it is for him to shift the weight, and the more likely it is he will be overweight or obese in adulthood.

Assessing your child

Studies show that most parents simply do not consider their children to be overweight, even when they are bordering on obesity. Thankfully, the UK government has recognised this and now supplies Body Mass Index charts in the health booklets given to every child at birth (see page 30 for more about BMI). Schools will also be helping parents keep tabs by monitoring growth (height and weight) annually.

BMI and children

From the age of one you can plot your child's BMI on a standard chart, which shows those of other children the same age. Because what is normal changes with age (young children have more 'baby fat', for instance), children's BMI measurements must be plotted on paediatric BMI charts rather than assessed using the normal range for adults. You use the same equation – weight in kilograms divided by height in metres squared – but on a different scale.

BMI declines from infancy to about five or six years of age, and then increases with age through childhood and adolescence. Kids tend to stick fairly closely to the same line throughout their childhood, and this is what you need to look at when working out if your child is obese: the real value of BMI measurements lies in viewing them as a pattern over time. For example, if your daughter shifts from the 50th to the 75th percentile, but remains there, she is probably growing in a way that is right for her. If you haven't kept a record of your child's weight and height across the years, you can start now.

Normal weight gain

It's also important to remember that many children do put on stores of fat in advance of a growth spurt, possibly during periods of illness, and always prior to and during adolescence. The distribution of weight also changes as children grow older. For example, from babyhood through to about five or six years of age, children accumulate more fat on their extremities than on their torsos. Then proportionally more fat accumulates around the tummy and trunk until adolescence. During the adolescent growth spurt, boys gain more fat on their trunks, while fat on their arms and legs decreases. Girls gain pretty much equal amounts of weight on their trunks, arms and legs during this period.

So the sudden appearance of a tummy after the age of six is not a sign of obesity, nor is this the case if your adolescent daughter suddenly develops more fat all over. It's worth remembering, too, that a child's body weight may double between the ages of 10 and 18.

Different shapes and sizes

Some kids are whippet-thin and others sturdier and more muscular. A stocky child is not any more likely to be overweight than a child with the physique of a budding ballerina. Accept your child's body shape, but be on the look-out for signs that all is not well. For example, if you regularly buy clothes two or three sizes larger than your child's age, or there are evident rolls of fat or hefty deposits on his body, chances are he does have weight problem.

Getting the balance right

An overweight child is susceptible to some pretty serious health problems, from diabetes and early heart disease to high blood pressure, among other things. Overlooking the problem at an early age can put your child in real danger of a lifetime of health problems. So do you put your child on a diet?

Definitely not. Dieting is a definite no-no for children – not only because it makes them feel 'different', but also because it teaches them nothing about long-term healthy eating habits and exercise – which are crucial to achieving balanced diets and healthy weight. The key is to keep his weight stable so that he 'grows into' a healthy way of life. Healthy living is the goal rather than watching the pounds fall off – but the wonderful byproduct is that he slims down.

The importance of exercise

The best and only way to ensure that your child's weight stabilises is exercise – lots of it, and on a regular basis – complemented by a healthy diet. The key thing to remember, however, is that if the whole family is involved, your child will be much more likely to sustain his efforts.

A programme that involves just one family member will never work – they'll lose the motivation required to keep things going, and they'll be made to feel 'different'. Children learn by example and then live what they learn. If everyone's doing it, good habits become a part of everyday life. Some say that ensuring that your child is more physically active instils a health benefit that is more powerful than medicine – and that's food for thought. So in this chapter I've designed a Six-Step Family Action Plan to help you accompany your child on their weight loss journey.

Each step has a task for both adults and children, so that the whole family works together to raise their physical activity and achieve their Energy Gap – improving both their fitness and their health. And just as you may experience challenges along the way on your own weight loss journey, so may your child. You'll find ideas to get them motivated, strategies to bash down barriers, and different types of activities for you to

choose together, just as you have made choices for yourself. Of course, what they are putting in their mouth is important, too. Later on in this chapter you'll find some tried and tested healthy eating tips, as well as some great meal ideas to tempt even the fussiest eaters.

The parental influence

The body weight of a biological parent is the most reliable predictor of your child's body weight in adulthood – your child's chances of becoming an overweight adult are 80 per cent greater if either you or your partner is overweight. But genes play only a small part – most experts agree that it is your actions and behaviour that have the most influence. So make sure you set a good example

How much exercise do children need?

The Chief Medical Officer recommends that children get a minimum of 60 minutes of at least moderate intensity physical exercise each day, plus activities designed to improve bone health, muscle strength and flexibility, at least twice a week. Currently 2 in 10 do less than 30 minutes of activity per day. Let's get planning how your children can meet the target.

Family Action Plan

1 Getting started

When it comes to taking action at home, there are several things you need to think about first of all. Before you grab your child to join you for a weekend jog across the park, bear in mind that children are not miniature adults – their physiological response to exercise is different.

Children's cardiovascular system is less like an endurance athlete and more like a sprinter. Their natural form of play is more stop-start, with short bursts of energy, so taking your children on a jog is physically more challenging for them and will make exercise seem a chore rather than something enjoyable. Stick with activities that suit their bodies.

Why not try:
- Sprinting games and races.
- Challenges, such as keeping a ball or balloon in the air.
- Games, such as It, Stuck-In-The-Mud, or Witches and Wizards.
- Sports, such as football, baseball, rounders, cricket or even roller-blading – anything that grabs their attention and keeps them moving.
- Taking short breaks when interest flags – play on the swings or slides, or go and feed the ducks.

Aim to be physically active with them for at least an hour.

If you don't have time...

The Henley Report, prepared by the American Physical Society, revealed that 85 per cent of the working population put in an atypical 9 to 5 day, with 37 per cent of parents working evenings and weekends (a figure that is, by 2020, set to double). If this is the case, as a parent you may need to think creatively about who can spend time with your children when you are unavailable.

One solution may be the grandparents, but if you don't have an extended family network nearby, it's important that you pass on your expectations to carers as well.

Consider enrolling your children in an after-school club or activity that focuses on sports or other active pursuits. Swimming lessons, Brazilian football skills classes, gymnastics, any form of dance, tennis coaching, circus skills for children, trampolining... the choices are endless. For the under-fives, you may find your local leisure centre runs a Tumble Tots class, which the little ones just love. Remember that every thing reinforces the type of behaviour you want to encourage! If they catch the exercise habit young, it will be much more likely that they'll grow up to be active – and healthy – adults.

Getting help

If your child is overweight or obese, it's important that you seek expert advice before undertaking any exercise programme or change in diet. A healthy diet is, by definition, one that excludes only unhealthy foods. And an exercise programme is designed to keep kids active rather than setting fitness targets that may be impossible to reach. Don't go to extremes. The vast majority of kids will thrive on your new family lifestyle.

However, some overweight children do have a physiological problem, and your GP should be your first port of call. If you are having trouble motivating your child to change his eating habits or to incorporate a little movement into his day, most surgeries have practice nurses who can help – and your doctor may also be able to refer you to one of the growing number of 'camps' and 'clubs' for overweight kids.

To find out more yourself, you may like to read a book called *How to Help Your Overweight Child* (2004) by Karen Sullivan, which is full of useful advice. Weight Concern (tel. 020 7679 6636; www.weightconcern.com) has useful advice on children's self-esteem and overcoming prejudice. The Institute of Child Health (020 7242 9789; www.ich.ucl.ac.uk) has a wealth of information on all kinds of health problems in children.

2 Ditch the sedentary alternatives

As a time-pressured parent, juggling work, family and home life, making or taking time out to exercise becomes a significant challenge. Exercise is often perceived as a pressure rather than a pleasure, and it slips further and further down the 'To Do' list. The situation is further compounded for parents, who confuse being physically active with being mentally or geographically active (see page 47). But whatever it is that is keeping you busy and making you tired, today's lifestyle is undeniably exhausting and the prospect of adding exercise to the equation may be more than daunting.

The influence of TV

Children, however, face a different challenge when it comes to physical activity. Their innate desire to move has been overshadowed by array of sedentary activities that we have often unthinkingly encouraged in an attempt to get a moment's peace. Children are particularly vulnerable to forms of media that require little physical involvement yet deliver strong sensory fulfilment, such as games consoles, computers, multi-channel television, mobile phone games and texting (and because of these, kids also tend to have short attention spans, flitting from one sedentary activity to the next).

Research has shown that outside of school, children are spending more time watching TV than any other activity other than sleeping – and the youngest children watch the most. One investigator surmised that simply decreasing a child's TV viewing by seven hours a week would reduce the risk of obesity by more than 30 per cent.

Family Activity Task

Find pockets of time in every 24-hour period in which you can all be more physically active. First complete the 24-hour Activity Chart opposite for each child (get them to do it with you if they're old enough). You may be surprised by what you discover. Studies have revealed we commonly overestimate how physically active we are by a whopping 51 per cent. Although you may have already filled in a chart for yourself in Chapter 3, do it again here so that your child feels that it is something you are doing together.

Next, identify the times you could add a period of at least 10 minutes of physical activity to the day. List all the family activities you plan to include.

Now, list all the sedentary activities that occupy your child, and brainstorm together to create a list of active alternatives. The purpose is not to remove all sedentary activities from your child's leisure time but instead provide a variety of both physical and non-physical activities to enjoy. And the emphasis must be on enjoyment. No child will willingly give up a Playstation session for something that's not as much fun!

Of all the activities you chose for yourself in Chapter 4, which ones can be undertaken as a family? Concentrate on those in the evenings and weekends when your child is not at school and let them join in. While it is important that your children see exercise as an integral part of your lifestyle, they are much more likely to want to be involved if your activities can easily be adjusted to include them.

Family Fit Fact: Thirst!

Children don't have an adult's ability to recognise thirst. In hot weather, after periods of activity, or even during a long day at school, they may be prone to dehydration, but they may mistake this for hunger and ask for food. Don't give them sweetened and fizzy drinks – they only add calories. If your child won't drink 'straight' water, try flavouring it with a little fresh orange or grape juice.

24-hour Activity Chart – kids

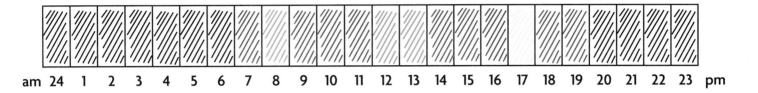

am 24   1   2   3   4   5   6   7   8   9   10   11   12   13   14   15   16   17   18   19   20   21   22   23   pm

Then colour:

- **Black** time spent lying down (this includes sprawling on the sofa)
- **Red** time spent on sedentary activities (in a vehicle, watching TV, playing on the computer or Playstation and even eating)
- **Orange** time they're on their feet (walking to and from school, for example)
- **Yellow** time spent doing strength training and resistance exercise (such as swimming)
- **Green** time spent in moderate intensity physical activity (such as brisk walking)
- **Purple** time spent doing vigorous exercise (such as a football match)

24-hour Activity Chart – parents

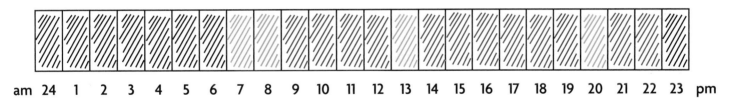

am 24   1   2   3   4   5   6   7   8   9   10   11   12   13   14   15   16   17   18   19   20   21   22   23   pm

Then colour:

- **Black** time spent lying down (this includes reading in bed, lying on the sofa)
- **Red** time spent on sedentary activities (at work, in a vehicle, watching TV, at a desk or computer, and even eating)
- **Orange**, time you're on your feet (such as doing the cooking or the housework)
- **Yellow** time spent doing strength or resistance work (include heavy manual lifting)
- **Green** time spent in moderate intensity physical activity (such as brisk walking)
- **Purple** time spent doing vigorous exercise (such as running)

3 Barrier Bashing for kids!

The barriers children come up against on their weight loss journey are completely different from the grown-up versions we've looked at. Instead, lack of self-esteem, poor body image and even boredom can stand in their way.

Family Activity Task

Identify your and your child's personal barriers to physical activity. If you've worked your way through this book, you're probably well aware of your own by now, but nevertheless completing this task together with your child can be a useful exercise. Remember: as a parent you are leading by example. Draw up a list of your barriers and brainstorm possible solutions for dealing with each barrier in a form like the one on the right. Here's an example of a possible barrier:

Barrier: Lack of self-esteem

Children may believe that they lack the skill required to exercise, or that their physical shape may hinder them. An obese child can feel uncomfortable about his body, and embarrassed about wearing exercise gear or swimming trunks. What's more, his size may make it harder for him to perform the activities required to expend energy.

Bash it down! Build in small victories, and nurture your child's Template of Success, as you do for yourself. But remember that while completing 120 seconds of activity 15 times a day may be a successful first step for you, for a child it will be meaningless – will-power is not a dominant characteristic in most kids, and they simply will not see the importance of doing something boring as a means to an end.

Family Barrier Bashing

Potential barriers to exercise for parents:

- -

Possible solutions for parents:

- -

Potential barriers to exercise for child

- -

Possible solutions for child

- -

Children need to feel that they are good at something, so don't push them in the direction of a sport they dislike and for which they have little talent. Think more along the lines of games in the park, a basketball or football match with friends or other families, roller-blading or a ride on the scooter, or even badminton or 'beach volleyball' in the garden. This will get them playing hard or running fast for 30–60 seconds and resting for a minute or two before carrying on – essentially mimicking alternate brief bouts of vigorous exercise with longer recovery periods.

Fit Family Fact: On your bike!

A young child is often less economical in her movements than an adult, but some modes of exercise can prove more effective for a child and hence build her self-confidence while she's still having fun. Cycling is one of the best all-round exercises a family can do together, because since it's independent of body weight and pedalling frequency (if the wheel size is the same), the mechanical efficiency of cycling is similar for children, adolescents and mums and dads! So plan a family cycling trip – why not bring a picnic and take a kite along?

4 Learning to love to move

One of the most important aspects of your child's future health is helping them learn to love to move – it provides a powerful foundation to make physical activity and exercise part of adult life. Central to this will be making movement and exercise fun, and building their physical confidence so they experience success. Developing this at as early an age as you can is vital. Get those toddlers dancing!

Family Activity Task

To help your child learn to love to move, the first thing is to avoid competition: start with games that focus on participation and fun rather than skill.

● Enjoy early success: as skilled activities are introduced it is important that children experience early success, otherwise enthusiasm will quickly fade. A child's success ratio can be easily improved by creatively alternating various aspects of a game, and can be tailored to achieve success for children of different abilities and ages in the family. Younger members can have more goes and head starts; older players can help younger players.

● Ensure the environment is non-threatening: arrange activities in the garden or as a family in the local park, rather than taking them somewhere they may feel awkward and on display. Try to make activities 'group' or 'family' orientated, rather than showcases for personal success.

● Variety is the spice of life: take a traditional game or sport and modify it in an unusual way.

Here are some suggestions:

● Try 'beach cricket'– allow a player more than three goes, increase the size of the bat or ball, reduce the size of the field or run length, or try to hit off a stationary bowler. Alternate these variables to suit each player, thereby keeping the interest level up as well as increasing each child's success ratio.

● Set up an obstacle course in the garden, and time yourselves. Ask each family member to create an obstacle!

● Crab football is a great leveller! All the players sit down on the playing field and use their arms and legs to move about instead of running. The size of the pitch will need to be significantly smaller, but all other rules can remain the same. Altering activities like this not only improves overall motor co-ordination and control but also makes it much more interesting and much more fun. What's more, previous experience or talent is likely to be useless!

● Arrange a scavenger hunt, which can be an ideal game for a child to enjoy with an older relative, or in a larger group within your community. Start them off by making a list of items for the children and the older adults to look for on a walk, such as a bottle top, or a leaf or flower of a particular size or colour. At the end of the walk the group with the most items selects the next adventure or gets to write the next list of items to search for.

● 'History walks' with a grandchild and grandparent can be a great way for different generations to spend quality time together. Grandparents can shed some light on the past while both generations get some exercise.

● Initiate family walking projects. Give each member of the family a pedometer and ask them to log their steps on a family chart. A certain number of steps equates to a certain mileage and you can add them all up to reach a chosen destination. Making an older child responsible for the step chart helps give them a sense of fulfilment and keeps Mum and Dad on track with their walking too! Out of interest, add up the mileage to try to reach different countries. Get the atlas and the encyclopaedia out and use this opportunity to educate your children about different cultures. Or perhaps reward the whole family with a fun day out once the destination is reached.

● Make activity a normal part of life – wash the car together, garden, mow the lawn, paint the house or the garden fence, clear the junk in the garden shed – anything that gets kids and adults up and out of the house. Give kids their own patch of garden to plant what they like.

● Set up a net in the garden and play badminton, volleyball or even 'tennis football' (keeping the ball in the air with feet and heads only). If the weather is bad, most kitchen tables can be easily turned into a table-tennis table.

● Have a sports day in the garden, complete with sack race, three-legged race and egg and spoon race!

● Have a water fight with water balloons, a paddling pool, a sprinkler and the garden hose. There's nothing that gets kids and adults moving more quickly than a little cold water!

Fit Family Fact: Children and heat

Children have a much lower capacity to dissipate heat during exercise. A child's individual sweat glands form sweat more slowly and are less sensitive to increases in core body temperature than those of adults. Encourage your child to begin slowly and take several activity breaks and ensure they are wearing comfortable, loose-fitting clothing that will keep them cool and make them less conscious of their figure.

5 Help kids to be successful

If you want your children to stick to exercise, they need to feel good about themselves. Your child's first exercise experience is crucially important in shaping their attitude to exercise. Getting it right can be like knocking down the first domino – when the first one topples the rest will follow.

● Use positive reinforcement ('If you ride your bike, you can go to the cinema on Saturday'). Reacting to inactivity with the threat of punishment is a sure way to turn a child off exercise.

● Avoid saying anything potentially derogatory. It can be extremely painful to be overweight.

● Develop trust. Overweight kids are wary of exercise – so trust is a must. Don't ask your child to do anything you would not be prepared to do yourself.

● Understand children's bodies: be aware of the physical differences (see page 206) when you plan your activities.

● Empower kids: focus on getting children to be comfortable with who they are now and encourage them to become who they want to be.

● Reward every week where weight doesn't increase with a (non-food) token of progress – such as a trip to the cinema, a CD or a family outing. Try to avoid rewards that reinforce sedentary behaviours, such as Playstation games.

● Talk to your children about what is realistic, and don't promise miracles. Stress the benefits of healthier living, and point out that maintaining weight is an added benefit, rather than the sole reason for staying active and eating well.

ructured

Having reg...
– or even...
planning t...
rather tha...
more, it te...
it, compet...

Streng...

Strength t...
nine or 10...
ligaments...
olds, bone...
those whe...
compared...
boosts th...
confidenc...
sustain du...
You'll nee...
this type...
child will...
safely, an...
rule of th...
designed...
warm-up...
three tim...

Yoga

Yoga is a...
navigate...
ease: it...
counter...
and imp...
coopera...
Physical...
body av...
class tha...
supervi...

6 Keep it going!

Children will undoubtedly become more excited about active play if they have the right equipment. Balls, shinpads, bats, racquets, frisbees, basketball nets, swings and other outdoor toys or games make great birthday gifts or even 'rewards'. Make sure your children have what they need to play the games they want to play.

But encourage, too, a little imaginary play in the garden or the park – finding the shiniest conker, making snow or sand 'angels', building a fort, climbing a tree, 'catching' butterflies or falling leaves – anything that imbues them with a sense of fun and adventure in the outdoors. The pleasure they experience will turn them into adults who will choose a country walk over a beer in front of the telly!

Fit Family Fact: How they move

Children and adolescents are a lot less economical in their movements than adults, using more oxygen per body weight than adults do at any given walking or running speed. So if you choose to jog together, enter a fun run, or weekend rambling activity, it is very important that your child sets the pace. Remember to praise them for being active, rather than criticising them for being slow. This changes the older they get – younger members of the family should not be expected to keep up with their older siblings.

Healthy eating for children

Exercise and activity are crucial to maintaining weight, and are an important part of a healthy lifestyle. But it goes without saying that the food your children eat is equally important.

Children should be encouraged to enjoy healthy food, and to get pleasure from the social experience of eating with friends and family. Good food keeps moods even, weight under control, helps them to learn and concentrate, encourages healthy growth and prevents disease. So healthy food should be a way of life, rather than a regime that is put into place every now and then. Remember: no child should ever be 'put on a diet'. It creates the wrong message and nurtures a Template of Failure.

Junk food

The temptation of junk food comes from all around them – not just from their friends but of course from advertising as well. But it's crucial that you combat it. Most importantly, remember that you are a crucial role model. If you relax with a packet of crisps, a chocolate bar and a glass of wine every evening, your kids will incite mutiny. Try to eat together, eat the same healthy foods, and keep the word 'diet' firmly away from your household.

We all like a treat from time to time, but you could help to redefine the word 'treat' if you're clever. Asparagus can be presented as a special dinner-time treat. A handful of ripe cherries and a little bowl to 'spit' the stones into is always popular. Multi-coloured vegetable crudités and their own little dish of dip will make many children happy.

Don't use the word 'treat' to define sweets or crisps. Instead, you could talk about 'sometimes' foods; explain that these are not everyday foods, because they're not very good for you, but that your child can have some from time to time so long as their diet is otherwise healthy. If you educate their tastebuds to enjoy fresh, natural tastes, they may even come to dislike the extremely salty or artificially sweet flavours of most types of junk food.

These tips are tried and tested on real families – and they work.

- Make meal time family time. Keep to set times as much as possible. Eat at the table, turn off the television and talk about what you all did that day.
- Go hands-on! Get the kids involved in preparing nutritious meals. From babyhood, children are fascinated by the texture, colour and taste of food, and when they're old enough you can help them be creative with it. Healthy pizzas, kebabs, fruit sticks and salads are all easily undertaken, even by little ones.
- Make healthy choices easy choices. Always keep the fruit bowl visible and easy to reach. Fill the snack cupboard with muesli bars, low-fat biscuits or fruit snacks.
- Search the supermarket. Food companies are bringing out new healthy food for children every month. Check food labels (see page 123) and make a list of good options. As a guideline, go for foods with less than 10g of fat and 15g of sugar per 100g. Watch out too for salt and sodium.
- Make all food family food. While kids will undoubtedly squawk for the same food their peers are eating (the ubiquitous chicken nuggets or turkey twizzlers, for example), they'll also take great pride in eating what mum and dad eat. Every family member should eat the same meals, and be encouraged to try new dishes from time to time.
- Survey school food. Find out what food choices are available at your child's school. Do they have healthy options you can include on lunch orders? Is the school part of a healthy canteens programme? Can parents get involved to help increase the number of healthy options?
- Watch the fat talk. Avoid making negative comments about your child's weight. Even sometimes seemingly endearing terms can be damaging. Curb their 'fat talk' too.

Practical food tips for parents

- Avoid using food as a reward for good behaviour.
- Don't choose unhealthy foods with a 'lower fat' or 'reduced sugar' content – they'll learn nothing about healthy eating if you serve the same junk with fewer unhealthy ingredients.
- Don't be tempted to go low-fat. Kids need fat to grow and develop. Simply serve a little less rather than low-fat brands.
- Praise good eating behaviours rather than scolding them about the negatives.
- Encourage at least a 'taste' of new healthy foods before kids leave the table. Acquiring a taste, rather than finishing the plate, may do more good in the long run.
- Don't give up on offering veggies at dinner. It may take 10 attempts to get kids to enjoy them, but it's worth it.
- Don't hesitate to get sneaky – sauces, stews, casseroles, pies, soups and even pastas are great hiding-places for grated or very finely chopped vegetables.
- Remember that fruit is a great source of vitamins and minerals too, plus the fibre that helps to keep weight at bay. Go with their favourite first.
- Cut fruit into small pieces that kids can pick at. You will be surprised at how quickly it gets gobbled up. Plums, cherries, strawberries and blueberries are bite-sized treats that can replace sweets.
- Offer small servings at first. They can always ask for more if they are hungry or love the taste. Downsize the food portions the whole family eats.
- Provide milk or juice at the end of meal times, so they don't get full before they eat.
- Make them a fruit platter for dessert if they are still hungry.
- Encourage water as a between-meals drink. Buy a water bottle with a superhero or whatever's 'cool' on it. Try to make one meal 'water plus food' only – so encouraging them to drink water rather than soft drinks and juice.
- Be creative. Make funny characters out of vegetables and cut sandwiches into shapes.
- Feed children dinner early before they get tired.
- Get Dad to eat his vegetables first and tell him to look as though he is enjoying them.
- Let relatives, friends or babysitters know what you expect your child to eat when they are in their care.

Healthy breakfasts

Serve all of the following with a glass of fresh juice.

High-fibre, low-sugar cereals served with milk or yoghurt, and topped with fruit (bananas and raisins are good choices).
Wholemeal toast with peanut butter or mashed bananas.
Boiled eggs with wholemeal toast soldiers.
Chopped fruit or compote with good-quality yoghurt.
Oatmeal or porridge with raisins and a little maple syrup for sweetening – add other dried fruits, seeds and nuts for variety.
A grilled lean bacon sandwich with tomatoes and sliced cucumbers, in wholemeal bread.
Rice cakes with apple slices and a slice of lean ham.
French toast – grilled, rather than fried. Brush it with a little melted butter to get that golden, crispy exterior.

Healthy snacks

Any of these will deal with between-meals hunger pangs.

Yoghurt
Fruit smoothies
Fruit salad
Fruit or vegetable skewer kebabs
Jelly fruit cups
Banana and dairy custard, sprinkled with cinnamon sugar
Vegetable sticks and dip
Air-popped popcorn
Wholemeal toast fingers with houmous or peanut butter
Rice cakes
Breadsticks
Cheese cubes

Healthy lunches at home

For weekends, school holidays or pre-schoolers.

Jacket potatoes with sun-dried tomatoes (see page 226).
Wholemeal toast with baked beans and grated cheese.

Wholemeal sandwiches, with a good-quality protein filling and salad – chicken, lean ham, turkey, boiled eggs, tuna, prawns or peanut butter are good choices.

Vegetable soups (purée them if the vegetables are a sticking point) with wholemeal bread or rice cakes, plus a little cheese.

Chicken legs or thighs with crudités.

Scrambled eggs on wholemeal toast with a glass of fresh juice and a piece of fruit.

Pasta with a light vegetable sauce and a sprinkling of cheese.

Grilled fish fingers with roasted homemade new potato 'chips' and crudités. (Or see the chips recipe on page 229.)

'Pizza' made on a wholemeal English muffin (or pitta, see page 226), with a smattering of cheese, a little tomato sauce and lots of crunchy vegetables.

Packed lunches

These are the bane of parents' lives – not only do you have to get the kids up, dressed, washed, homeworked and off on time, but you have to provide something nutritious and filling for them as well. And there's nothing worse than looking in the lunchbox when they come home and realising that they've only eaten half of its contents – or finding out from another mother that your child's been giving their lunch away.

There is a lot of peer pressure at school, and you will be faced with constant demands for crisps and chocolates with the insistence that 'everyone else has them'. A quick playground survey will probably confirm that this isn't true.

Here are some tips:

Sandwiches If your child won't eat anything except jam in her sandwich, make sure the bread is wholemeal and that you give her a source of protein to keep her feeling full (see below). Choose a low-sugar, high-fruit preserve instead of sugary jams. Fruits and vegetables of some description will round off the meal.

Fruit and vegetables Go for apples and pears, or easy-peel clementines or satsumas, as oranges can be a hassle to peel and off-puttingly messy. Kids may prefer to eat fruit that has been quartered and cored (put it in a plastic container) – especially if they are losing teeth and can't bite properly. You can substitute a chunk of cucumber, some carrot sticks, a few cherry tomatoes or some sliced red pepper for fruit.

If the fruit isn't eaten at the end of the day, you can insist that it gets eaten before a teatime snack of biscuits or cakes. At teatime, put a plate of chopped fruit on the table when they come back from school. If they finish that they'll probably forget about wanting biscuits or cake; and if you eat a piece of fruit at the same time it helps to reinforce the message that fruit is a snack in itself.

Protein It's important to keep protein intake up during the day, so here are some suggestions:

● Tuna mayonnaise in a pot, with breadsticks or carrot sticks to dip in.

● A hard-boiled egg.

● A couple of rashers of grilled bacon (or a bacon sandwich).

● Cooked chicken chunks mixed with a little mayonnaise and sweetcorn, put in a pot with breadsticks or cucumber chunks to dip.

● A slice of ham, spread with cream cheese and rolled into a cigar (you can add a chopped prune, or a chunk of canned pineapple, drained and finely chopped).

● Two water biscuits sandwiched together with cream cheese (squeeze them together and watch the cheese spurt out of the holes).

● Angels on horseback (a rasher of streaky bacon wrapped around a stoned prune, and secured with a cocktail stick, baked for 8 minutes in a hot oven). These keep in the fridge for a day or two (don't forget to remove the stick!).

Healthy dinners

Serve whatever you are having, or choose one of the following nutritionally balanced favourites.

Grilled chicken breasts or roasted chicken legs with baked potatoes or new potatoes, green beans, broccoli and carrots.

Lean sausages with baked beans, rice or new potatoes and sliced cucumber.

Any roasted meat or poultry with steamed potatoes or rice, and plenty of fresh vegetables (raw or cooked).

Chilli con carne with rice or a baked potato and salad.

Spaghetti bolognese and salad (or crudités, which kids tend to like more in my experience).

Any wholewheat pasta with a vegetable-based sauce and plenty of colourful crudités.

Lean meat or poultry stir-fry, with honey and a little soya sauce, plus any combination of vegetables and rice.

Chicken strips, dipped in egg and then wholemeal breadcrumbs and grilled, served with fresh vegetables and rice or new potatoes (or see the recipe on page 229).

A big bowl of vegetable soup with wholegrain bread, cheese and vegetable crudités.

Pork chops with apple sauce, roasted potatoes (par-boil them first, drizzle with olive oil and roast), served with any combination of vegetables.

Lasagne, substituting ricotta or cottage cheese for the béchamel sauce, and topping with only a little grated cheese, with salad or crudités.

Roasted Mediterranean vegetables with couscous and a little crumbled feta cheese.

Turkey or chicken breasts grilled with lemon and herbs, served on a wholemeal bun with crudités or salad.

Homemade burgers with crudités and homemade chips.

Homemade pizza (see page 226) with crudités.

Fajitas – strips of chicken, beef or turkey sautéed in a little olive oil with chilli seasoning, onions and peppers, served in a wholegrain tortilla wrap with sautéed red and yellow peppers and a little salsa. (Let them roll their own.)

Salmon fillets or tuna steaks, served with new potatoes and any combination of vegetables.

Fish pie – cod, prawns or tuna can be added to chopped boiled potatoes and steamed vegetables – served in a sauce made from boursin cheese (or another soft cheese made with herbs) and a little milk and fish stock. Top with sunflower seeds and bake.

Chicken cordon bleu – flatten a boneless chicken breast, lay a slice of lean ham and a slice of cheese in the centre, roll and secure with a little cotton. Sauté lightly in a little olive oil to seal, and then bake in the oven until cooked, with some white wine and stock. Serve with salad and rice. Kids love it and it's a low-fat version of breaded Kiev-type chicken dishes.

Stews and casseroles with plenty of vegetables and lean meats, cooked with some wine, herbs and stock, which will naturally thicken when reduced. Serve with a wholegrain roll or rice, plus some salad.

When it comes to food, we all know that children have very strong dislikes. But equally, they often develop a taste for the most unexpected foods! Don't be overcautious. Look through the recipes in Chapter 5 and pick out some to try on the whole family. Also, don't forget the firm favourites. On the next pages are just a few dishes children will love to help you make.

Recipes

Banana-chocolate smoothie

calories 191.50   **fat** 4.08   **protein** 8.88   **carbohydrates** 32.60

A delicious way to start the day – and a great means of getting breakfast into children.

Serves 2 Prep time: 3 minutes Cooking time: none
150g low-fat bio live yoghurt
300ml semi-skimmed milk
2 heaped tsp drinking chocolate
2 ripe bananas, sliced, or 100g fruit (see below)

1 Put the yoghurt, milk, drinking chocolate and banana (or fruit) into a blender. Whizz on high speed for 30 seconds, until smooth.

Play around with the fruit combinations. Alternatives are:
100g strawberries and 2 tsp drinking chocolate
100g raspberries and 2 tsp drinking chocolate
1 ripe mango and a few sprigs of fresh mint to decorate
100g stewed apricots and some chopped lemon zest

Banana-sour cherry bread

calories 282.38   **fat** 10.32   **protein** 3.67   **carbohydrates** 45.18

This is very good toasted for breakfast or between-meal snacks. It can be frozen with pieces of baking parchment between each slice so that you can defrost it a piece at a time. A tasty treat that's healthy as well!

Serves 6–8 Prep time: 10 minutes Cooking time: 1 hour
225g plain flour
1 tsp salt
1 heaped tsp baking powder
1 tsp ground cinnamon
110g caster sugar
1 egg, beaten
90g unsalted butter, melted
a few drops vanilla essence
90g dried sour cherries
3 very ripe bananas, mashed

1 Preheat the oven to 180°C/350°F/Gas Mark 4. Sift together the flour, salt, baking powder and cinnamon. Stir in the sugar. With a fork, mix in the egg, melted butter and vanilla essence. Add the mashed bananas and cherries and mix with a fork just until all the ingredients are incorporated: don't overmix.

2 Spoon the mixture into the prepared tin and bake for 50–60 minutes until the loaf springs back when prodded. Leave in the tin for 10 minutes before turning it out to cool.

Stuffed baked potatoes with sun-dried tomatoes

calories 286.50   **fat** 10.71   **protein** 14.47   **carbohydrates** 33.64

The concentrated flavour of the sun-dried tomatoes means you don't need any additional salt on your potatoes. This dish works well as a family lunch with a green salad or a selection of steamed vegetables when the weather is colder.

Serves 4 Prep time: 10 minutes Cooking time: 1 hour
4 x 125g baking potatoes
1 sun-dried tomato per person
100g low-fat Cheddar cheese, chopped into small chunks
25g healthy margarine
50g grated Parmesan cheese

1 Bake the potatoes – if you microwave them on high for at least 5 minutes at the beginning you won't end up with crunchy uncooked middles. Alternatively, you can cook them all the way through in the microwave (turning them regularly), before transferring them to the oven for 15 minutes at 200°C/400°F/Gas Mark 4 to crisp up the skins.

2 While they are baking, prepare the filling by chopping the sun-dried tomatoes very finely, and mixing them with the cheese chunks.

3 When the potatoes are done, cut them in half and carefully scoop out the flesh, reserving the skins. (Use oven gloves so you don't tear the skins.) Mash the flesh with the margarine in a bowl, then mix in the sun-dried tomato and cheese chunks. Pile the stuffings into the potato skins.

4 Place the filled skins in a baking dish (use scrunched up tinfoil to keep them upright in the oven). Sprinkle with grated Parmesan. Return to the oven for 5 minutes before serving.

Pitta bread pizzas

calories 319   **fat** 8.84   **protein** 18.4   **carbohydrates** 41.27

This is the really easy way to make pizzas, and it's fun for kids because they can choose and arrange their own toppings. There is very little fat if you make them this way, and you can keep pitta breads on hand in the freezer. To make pizzas from frozen pitta bread, increase the cooking time by 2 minutes.

Serves 4 Prep time: 5–10 minutes Cooking time: 8 minutes
1 x 410g tin chopped tomatoes
1 tsp dried mixed herbs (or 1/2 tsp each of thyme and oregano)
8 regular or 4 large white pitta breads

Toppings:
Choose from olives, thinly sliced red or green peppers, a couple of rounds of salami cut into thin strips, wafer thin ham, small chunks of canned pineapple. For more adult tastes, try a few thin slices of aubergine, some sliced mushrooms, anchovies, or a teaspoon of pesto sauce.

200g grated low-fat mozzarella cheese

1 Preheat the oven to 230°C/450°F/Gas Mark 6. Mix the herbs with the chopped tomatoes in a small bowl, and then spread thinly on each of the pitta breads. Add a selection of toppings, then sprinkle the grated mozzarella over the top.

2 Bake for 8 minutes or until the cheese is golden brown. It's as simple as that!

Healthy chicken nuggets with easy baked chips

calories 475   **fat** 29   **protein** 22.31   **carbohydrates** 31.17

If only all chicken nuggets were made this way… And if only all chips actually tasted of the potatoes they are made of, instead of the fat they're fried in. It's a good idea to make several batches of the nuggets as they freeze very well: I freeze them, either on a baking tray in one layer, or layered with baking parchment so they don't stick together. Then I bag them up in Ziploc bags, and can shake them out onto the baking tray and whip them into the oven when I need them.

Remember that if you use frozen chicken breast, it needs to be thoroughly defrosted before you cook it, and you must cook the nuggets before freezing them.

Serves 4 Prep time: 15 minutes Cooking time: 30 minutes
For the nuggets
2 x 200g chicken breasts, skin removed and chopped into
  bite-sized chunks
4 tbsp plain flour
2 large eggs, beaten with 2 tbsp water
2 Weetabix, crumbled fine, or 6 tbsp dry breadcrumbs
6 tbsp vegetable oil
1/4 tsp paprika
a pinch of salt
few grindings black pepper

For the chips
4 x 200g large roasting potatoes
2 tbsp vegetable oil
a pinch of salt

1 Preheat the oven to 200°C/400°F/Gas Mark 6. Cut the potatoes in half along their length, and cut these into thin wedge shapes. Spray them with the vegetable oil and lightly sprinkle a little salt on them. Arrange the potato wedges on one end of the baking tray, and cook for 15 minutes.

2 While the chips are cooking, set up your production line: you will want a plastic bag with no holes in it, three bowls and a piece of baking parchment. Have the bowl with the egg and water mix on the left (or right, if you're left-handed), then the bowl with the breadcrumbs or crumbled Weetabix, then the bowl with the vegetable oil, then a piece of baking parchment. Put the flour and the chicken chunks into the plastic bag, and shake vigorously until all the chicken is well coated. Place this bag on the far side of the bowl with the water and egg mixture.

3 Take a floured chicken chunk, roll it quickly in the egg mix, then in the Weetabix crumbs until it's well coated, then spray it with the oil, and place it on the baking parchment. Repeat with the rest of the chunks.

4 After the chips have had 15 minutes in the oven, remove the baking tray and flip the chips over with a spatula. Add the chicken nuggets to the tray and return to the oven for 15 minutes until everything is golden brown.

Now that you have all the tools you will need to lose weight, the time has finally come for you to put them into practice.

Remember that as you set out on your weight-loss journey, it's important to be realistic about what you can achieve. There may never be a 'perfect time' for you to begin your action plan, so don't wait for the perfect time – in my experience, if you adopt this attitude you'll never get past the starting line.

Your long-term success will depend upon how well you navigate your time from now on, and how you choose to live your life.

If you have the desire to lose weight and are willing to put in some effort, you will succeed. Remember that each small step you take along the way will make a big difference.

You can do this! Go for it!

questions & answers

"The diet I'm following is very low carb (just two slices of wholegrain bread allowed three times a week). I've lost 17 pounds in 7 weeks and would like to lose another 30 pounds over the next 3 months, but do I need more in the way of carbs?"

Congratulations on all of your hard work! Realistic and healthy goal setting is an important part of the weight loss process. If we set unrealistic goals, it can backfire and de-motivate us and re-inforce your Template of Failure – not what we want. A realistic and healthy weight loss goal is about 5 to 10 per cent of your current body weight in 3 to 6 months.

Watch the calories, not the carbs
It sounds as though your diet is focusing on healthy foods, but it would be a good idea to include some wholegrain starches every day, both for the fibre and for the B vitamins they provide. This shouldn't affect your rate of weight loss if you remember it is calories and not carbs that cause people to gain weight. Wholegrain cereal, crackers, pasta, bread, brown rice and low-fat popcorn are delicious and nutritious when eaten in moderation and operating my Carb Curfew is a useful way to keep your quantities in check.

"Because of my shift I eat late at night when I get home. What's the absolute latest I should be eating, and are there foods I should avoid so as not to tax the digestive system before I go to bed?"

Try to eat about one to two hours before you go to bed to allow your food to digest. Be sure to eat slowly and chew your food very well – digestion begins in the mouth, with the action of saliva.

Keep it simple
We are often tense or tired when we eat late at night, which can make us vulnerable to overeating. Use a small plate to remind yourself to eat smaller portions, and make sure that half of your plate is filled with colourful fruits and vegetables. Avoid spicy, fatty foods late at night, or those with rich, creamy sauces. Keep it simple – opt for soups and salads rather than an Indian takeaway.

> According to an online calorie counter, I should be eating between 1,755 and 2,025 calories a day to reach my goal. I'm only eating 1,400 but my weight loss has stalled. Am I eating too little?

Yes, that could be the case. When you're eating too few calories, your body gets a signal that you're starving, and all of your systems – your cardiovascular system, nervous system, gastrointestinal system, endocrine system – slow down, so that you're burning fewer calories and are better able to survive the 'famine'.

Count your calories carefully

I suggest that no one eats less than 1,500 calories a day except under medical supervision. But before you start eating more, make sure that you're counting everything you eat and drink accurately. If you're eating the right amount of calories and still not losing weight, see your doctor to check if you have metabolic problems.

> I think my friend may have anorexia. She has lost a lot of weight recently and she makes excuses not to eat out with her friends, saying she'll join us afterwards. What should I do?

Anorexia nervosa is a disorder characterised by extreme weight loss and an intense fear of being fat. The disorder occurs most commonly in adolescent girls, but it is becoming more common in young men. People suffering from anorexia are very skinny and have often lost as much as a third of their body weight. They may exercise compulsively, and grow soft downy hair all over their body.

Get specialist help

If you suspect someone has an eating disorder such as anorexia or bulimia (a disorder in which sufferers binge eat and then induce vomiting), they need a lot of specialist support. Talk to your friend, but be prepared for denial and resistance. It may be helpful to contact the Eating Disorders Association (www.edauk.com, tel: 0845 634 1414); they will be able to give you advice on how to handle the situation.

> When I first started exercising I lost weight quickly. Why can't I drop the last few pounds?

So you have lost the 'easy weight' – now comes the hard part! On any weight loss programme the greatest changes generally occur early on; and heavier, less fit people get more dramatic results at first. The closer you are to the last 2kg (5lb), the more effort you are going to have to put in.

Track your pulse

Trying a new activity can bring your resting pulse up, causing your body to burn more calories. Keep a tab on your resting pulse, as if it drops it could be a sign to shift your cardio training regime. Do some interval training at two sessions a week to trigger surges of growth hormone that promote fat burning. Maybe you should also do a reality check: the last 2kg (5lb) may be the hardest to lose because you are actually trying to get below your ideal weight. Read pages 30–3 for ways of judging what your healthy weight and shape should be.

> Help! I've got cellulite! Can I get rid of it with diet and exercise?

Most experts agree cellulite is in part genetic, so the first thing I would suggest you do is take a look at the women in your family. However, your diet, exercise levels and body beauty routine can all affect the appearance of cellulite on your hips and thighs. Longer term, regular cardio exercise and decreasing the toxic load in your body by cutting back on processed foods and additives has been reported by some individuals to make a difference.

Get exercising

I suggest you introduce an interval cardio programme with 3-minute cardio bouts interspaced with compound large muscle group exercises, such as the Four-point Lunge (page 94), or the Can Opener and Extension (page 88). I would also suggest you try to minimise your alcohol and caffeine intake and cut right back on any artifical flavourings.

Body brushing

Some of my clients swear by rubbing a few drops of sweet fennel essential oil into their body moisturiser and rubbing in light upward sweeping movements on hips, thighs and bottom. You should also try dry body brushing before each shower. Sweep towards the groin lymph nodes to aid lymph drainage.

> I try to eat as well as I can, but recently I have been bingeing on junk food late at night for no reason. I exercise regularly and eat well the rest of the time. How can I stop myself bingeing?

It seems on the surface that you are doing the right things in your diet and exercise, but you are not in the right head space! Although you are exercising, your brain seems to expect you to fail and let yourself down. Have you followed a lot of different diets in the past, especially extreme quick-fix ones? In my experience, this can cause low self-esteem; you start to doubt that your actions will work.

Build a Template of Success

To do this I suggest you pick three small things that can be building blocks each week to help you towards your goal. For example, operate my Carb Curfew after 5pm; just say no to bread, pasta, rice and potatoes and instead focus your evening meal on lean meat, fish, fruit and veg with some essential fats. This will help you to cut down your calorie intake and will also reduce bloating. On top of this, be sure to drink your 2 litres of water a day, and take a brisk 10-minute walk before you sit down at your desk. All these small actions add up and help you build a Template of Success! Look at the 7 Steps to Self Esteem on pages 18–19 to help analyse your attitude further.

I do loads of sit-ups but I still have a jelly belly — what am I doing wrong?

Sit-ups are technically a toning exercise designed to challenge the abdominal group of muscles. Performing sit-ups with good technique will help to tighten, flatten and strengthen your abdominals. However these muscles lie under a layer of adipose (fat) tissue. If you are not over-eating, the excess abdominal fat may be a sign of too much tension and stress. Long-term chronic stress that goes unchecked creates a build-up of the stress hormone cortisol. Cortisol creates a challenge to weight loss on two levels: first it increases appetite, especially the urge for sugary sweets, and second it encourages these excess calories to be laid down around the midriff area.

Add sweat to your sit-ups

Any vigorous exercise helps reduce overall body fat, including that tummy. While it was once thought we were born with a certain number of fat cells, scientists now believe that once our existing fat cells reach a critical size they split, creating more fat cells. To keep the fat off your midriff you need to make cardio exercise a regular feature of your training programme.

Control your stress

Try to build a stress reducer into your daily life — this will be different for each of us, but yoga, listening to relaxing music, enjoying a soothing bath and walking can be great stress reducers, which will help regulate your cortisol levels and keep that belly bulge at bay. Getting enough good quality sleep is important too; studies have shown getting 6 versus 8 hours of sleep increases cortisol output by 40 per cent.

Ban the booze

Alcohol is very calorie dense. Every gram contains 7 calories, almost twice as much as protein and carbohydrates. In addition research shows that some types of alcohol — mainly beer — can cause more fat to settle on your belly.

My friend and I eat and exercise the same, yet she's only the one losing weight. Why her and not me? It's just not fair.

To get the answer to this one, you need to look at your parents. If you had an overweight parent then you have a 79 per cent greater chance of having weight problems as an adult. (Your chances are slightly higher if it was your Mum.) Genetics affect our shape and how our bodies respond to food and exercise by as much as 40 per cent. But before you toss in the towel remember that your DNA is not your destiny. The most effective change you can make is to become a regular exerciser and make it a consistent five-times-a-week habit. If you burn an extra 30 calories an hour during the 14 to 16 hours that you are awake — by taking the stairs or walking briskly instead of dawdling — you could incinerate up to 500 extra calories a day without doing an actual workout. You could even overtake your friend!

glossary

Abdominals – the group of muscles at the front of the body. Commonly referred to (though incorrectly) as tummy muscles.

Adipose tissue – fatty, connective tissue made up of fat cells. Found directly under the skin and around the delicate organs of the body.

Adrenal glands – orange-coloured endocrine glands, located on the top of both kidneys. They produce epinephrine and norepinephrine (adrenaline), the hormones active during stress and exercise.

Aerobic capacity – refers to the body's ability to consume oxygen at cellular level and produce energy.

Alcohol, unit of – a unit of alcohol is 10ml of pure alcohol. For recommended intake limits, see page 119.

Amino acids – nitrogen-containing compounds that are the building blocks of protein.

Anorexia nervosa – an eating disorder characterised by an intense fear of becoming fat. Sufferers experience a distorted body image and extreme weight loss. The condition is associated with self-starvation, often creating metabolic abnormalities, and seriously detrimental to health.

Blood pressure – the pressure exerted by the blood on the walls of the arteries, measured in millimetres of mercury by a sphygmomanometer.

Body Mass Index – a relative measure of body height to body weight for determining degrees of obesity (see page 30).

Break-point walking – the way I recommend you walk – see page 69.

Bulimia – an eating disorder characterised by episodes of binge eating followed by fasting, self-induced vomiting or the use of diuretics or laxatives. It can severely damage your health.

Calorie – or kilocalorie (kcal) is the amount of heat energy needed to raise the temperature of 1 kilogram of water by 1°C, commonly used as a measure of energy in food.

Carb Curfew – means no bread, pasta, rice, potatoes or cereal after 5pm.

Carbohydrates (simple and complex) – essential nutrients that provide energy to the body. Dietary sources include sugars (simple) and grains, rice, potatoes and beans (complex). 1gm carb = 4 kcals. For more info, see page 103.

Cardiovascular exercise (cardio) – involves moving your body with the use of the large muscle groups. Uses oxygen as a source of energy, so it strengthens the heart, lungs and circulatory system.

Cellulite – a non-medical term often used to describe subcutaneous fat, commonly found in the thighs and buttocks, that appears dimpled like orange peel.

Cholesterol – a fatty substance found in the blood and body tissues and in animal products. Essential for the production of certain hormones but its accumulation leads to narrowing of the arteries (atherosclerosis).

Diabetes – a disease of carbohydrate metabolism in which an absolute or relative deficiency of insulin results in an inability to metabolise carbohydrates normally.

Energy Gap – burning more calories through activity than you take in through your food and drink. The only way to lose weight!

Extension – movement at a joint bringing two parts into or toward a straight line, thereby increasing the angle of the joint. An example might be straightening the arm. It's the opposite of flexion (qv).

Fats (saturated, polyunsaturated, monounsaturated, trans/hydrogenated) – an essential nutrient that provides energy, energy storage and insulation to the body. 1gm fat = 9 kcals. For more info, see page 105.

Fibre – dietary fibre is mainly derived from plant cell walls. There are two types: soluble and insoluble (see page 108).

Flexion – movement about a joint in which the bones on either side of the joints are brought closer to each other. An example might be bending the arm. It's the opposite of extension (qv).

Genes – units carried on a chromosome that control transmission of hereditary characteristics and consist of DNA and RNA.

Glucose – a simple sugar; the form in which all carbohydrates are used as the body's principal energy source.

Glycogen – the form in which glucose is stored in the liver and muscles.

Glycaemic Index – classifies a food by how high and for how long it raises blood glucose levels.

Heart-rate monitor – consists of a chest strap that contains electrodes that pick up the actual heart rate (not pulse rate) and transmit the signal to a digital readout on a wrist receiver.

Hormones – chemical messengers that are synthesised, stored in and released into the blood by endocrine glands.

Hydration – the amount of water in the body.

Hypertension – high blood pressure (above 140/90mmHg).

Hypothalamus – section of the brain primarily responsible for linking its communication with the body.

Insulin – a hormone that helps the body utilise blood glucose.

Insulin resistance – occurs when the normal amount of insulin secreted by the pancreas is not able to maintain normal blood glucose levels. When the body cells resist or do not respond to even high levels of insulin, glucose builds up in the blood resulting in high blood glucose or even type 2 diabetes.

Intensity of exercise – the physiological stress on the body during exercise. Indicates how hard the body should be working to achieve a training effect.

Interval training – short, high-intensity exercise periods alternated with periods of rest or less intensive active recovery. For example, a 100-yard run then a 1-minute rest, repeated eight times.

Lactic acid – a waste product of anaerobic energy production known to cause localised muscle fatigue.

Menopause – cessation of menstruation in the human female, usually occurring between the ages of 45 and 55.

Metabolism – the chemical and physiological processes in the body that provide energy for the maintenance of life.

Neutral position – with the lumbar spine and pelvis in the central position, not flexed, extended, tilted or rotated. Thought to be the best position for good posture.

Nutrients (and micronutrients) – life-sustaining substances found in food. They supply the body with energy and structural materials and regulate growth, maintenance and repair of the body's tissues.

Obliques – part of the abdominal muscles (qv). The obliques lie on a diagonal in the torso, forming your waist.

Omega 3 fatty acids – a form of fat, found mainly in oily fish and flax and pumpkin seeds.

Oestrogen – one of the female hormones that helps regulate a woman's passage through menstruation, fertility and menopause.

Pedometer – a simple device you attach to your belt. It records each step through a sensory device registering motion at the hip.

Perceived rate of exertion (PRE) – method used to regulate intensity (qv) during aerobic endurance training. Rating is recorded numerically by your own perception of how hard you are working

Peri-menopause – the stage leading into full menopause (qv). This can begin up to eight years before full menopause.

Portion Distortion – a term I use to describe over-generous serving sizes of food, for example on manufacturers' packaging.

Probiotics – these are commonly ingested as bacteria in live yoghurt to enhance the intestinal flora and so aid digestion.

Resistance exercise – involves exerting a force to enable you to move or apply tension to a weight and results in enhanced muscular strength and endurance.

Resting metabolic rate – the number of calories expended per unit time when you are at rest. It is measured early in the morning after an overnight fast and at least 8 hours of sleep.

Rib-hip connection – this helps with abdominal contraction before lifting and ensures the correct anatomical position of the spine.

Strength training – see resistance exercise (qv).

Structured exercise – involves putting on your trainers, setting aside specific time to take exercise and getting a little bit hot and sweaty.

Thermic effect of food – is the increase in energy expenditure above the resting metabolic rate as a result of eating a meal.

Thermic effect of exercise – is the energy expended in physical activity.

Thermogenesis – increased energy expenditure for heat production.

Testosterone – the male sex hormone (although women have testosterone levels one-tenth to one-twelfth of those of men).

Weight-bearing exercise – exercise that tones and uses your own body weight, such as Pilates and yoga.

stockists

Tanita Body Fat Scales and Skipping Ropes www.tanita.com

Joanna Hall pedometers www.pedometersuk.co.uk

Sweaty Betty for exercise clothing www.sweatybetty.com

She Active for exercise clothing www.sheactive.co.uk

Juicers www.ukjuicers.com

See also the **Sustrans** website (www.sustrans.org.uk), where they set out a blueprint for walking and cycling in London.

index

acknowledgments

Putting together *The Weight Loss Bible* has involved a huge amount of support from loved ones, from my fabulous friends and some wonderful professional colleagues. Working on this project has involved smiles, sweat, stress, lots of giggles and even a few tears from one or two of our younger models. But without them, this book would not have been possible. So I am extremely grateful to everyone involved.

Turning each page brings special memories of the clients who have inspired me with their weight loss efforts and all the great people involved in bringing the book together.

Thanks go to the team on the front line: Vanessa Courtier for a fabulous creative design and my editor Gill Paul for her ability to share my vision, her patience and continual skill to keep the whole project on track; Jane Tyler for her ability to tame my mane and makeup, through all winds and weathers; Louise Shaxson for the delicious recipes; David Morgan and Angela Boggiano for the salivating food styling; Wei Tang for prop styling; and, of course, the whole team at my publishers Kyle Cathie, especially Vicki Murrell, Julia Barder and Kyle herself.

Many of my friends and clients have put themselves out to help and be photographed, and I am so grateful for their support. My Westover House Weight Management Course ladies happily agreed to be photographed during our exceedingly early morning training sessions on fresh-weathered March mornings. The aqua class at the Royal Free Recreation Club, run by Cheryl Burns, were a total inspiration and a delight to watch, and Luke Courtier kindly let us photograph him at Guy McDouall's Thai boxing class in the Armoury, North London. Thanks also to Peter Ottevanger for allowing us to take photos in Pilates Central.

Our younger models came from the Shepherd and Bonnel families, and it would be most remiss of me if I did not name them all personally: Max, Henry, the twins Phoebe and Lydia, Imogen, Olivia, George and Felix. Thanks also for the energetic modelling skills of Mr and Mrs Shepherd and Mr and Mrs Bonnell. Lucy and Nick Riley and Emily Corner made their colourful juicing creations on my great friend Sophie's birthday weekend at the Riley home. My dear friend Bethan, who has run with me in more than a few fabulous destinations across Europe and the US, whizzed over between business meetings to be photographed as we ran at lunchtime on Primrose Hill. My friends Karen and Danila are remarkable for their perpetual party and culinary skills. Of course, being totally biased – as only an aunt can – I'd like to thank my very special niece Georgia Hall, who has her cartwheeling down to a fine art.

Last, but by no means least, one person made all of this possible. The photographer Dan Welldon, who is also my partner, provides unending personal support to me and is a constant source of inspiration.

Small Steps Big Changes

I have been using pedometers with my clients for more than six years and have found them to be the number one piece of equipment you need, whether you want to improve your health, your fitness or to walk off your weight. Over the years I've come across a lot of different pedometers and some of them – while looking good or perhaps being free – are unreliable and inaccurate, meaning all your walking effort is not giving your body the results and health benefits it needs and deserves. That's why in association with UK Pedometers I developed my own model, called Joanna's Small Steps Big Changes pedometer. Carrying the Gold Standard for research, this pedometer is accurate and simple to use; there's no need to measure your step length; and it comes in a variety of colours. There are two models, one measuring your steps and one measuring steps and time. Now you can wear Joanna's pedometer, confident in the knowledge that it is tracking your health every step of the way. You can order my pedometer direct from www.pedometersuk.co.uk